# THE SACRAMENTALITY OF PERSONHOOD

## A PHILOSOPHICAL THIRST MEETS THEOLOGY

Msgr. Walter R Oxley

En Route Books and Media, LLC
Saint Louis, MO

ENROUTE

Make the time

En Route Books and Media, LLC
5705 Rhodes Avenue
St. Louis, MO 63109

Cover credit: Sebastian Mahfood


ISBN-13: 979-8-88870-401-1
Library of Congress Control Number: 2025943571

## Table of Contents

Dedicated to Pope Leo XIV,
the First Pope from the United States of
America

# Foreword

It gives me great pleasure to write this foreword for Msgr. Oxley's new text on philosophy's contribution to theology. I have known Msgr. Oxley for almost 30 years, first in the seminary and then as a trusted colleague and friend on the formation at that same seminary, the Pontifical North American College. Msgr. Oxley is a man of the Church and, as such, it is fitting that he writes about a tradition of the Church, namely the function of philosophy within theology.

I myself have had a mixed relationship with philosophy. As a minor seminarian in the early 1990s, I became a philosophy major in college by accident. As it turned out, I was a English major who also took an awful lot of philosophy courses, mostly so I could have one as my professor a truly fine priest, Fr. Robert Lauder, at New York's Saint John's University. The dean of the Philosophy department asked me if I would declare a philosophy major so that I could win the Silver Key as a graduating senior. So, I graduated with a BA as a double-major in English and Philosophy.

Now, just because I studied a great deal of philosophy on the undergraduate level doesn't mean that I really learned much. Sure, I had some wonderful professors who guided me through some very important classes- philosophical anthropology, ethics, epistemology, metaphysics, ancient, modern, contemporary, American, existentialism, personalism, philosophy of literature, and Problem of God. I learned a great deal and I owe so much to these professors. However, note what classes I did not list above- logic, Medieval philosophy, and Thomism. This was a major lacunae.

The main philosopher whom I studied was Bernard Lonergan, a transcendental Thomist (and, as it happened, I eventually would write my doctorate on Lonergan, which I adapted into A Concise Introduction to Bernard Lonergan, SJ, published in 2025 by En Route). But there were glaring errors of which I was completely unaware until I began my own doctoral studies in theology at the Angelicum in Rome.

When I started at the Angelicum, I felt like, to use a metaphor, a dog watching television. Surrounded by fine Dominican friars, it was as if I needed to know the Summa, Aristotle, Duns Scotus, Bonaventure, Augustine, Plato like it was essential to do dogmatic and fundamental theology! Eventually, I would leave the Angelicum and go over to the Gregorian University to complete my doctorate, but, in the meantime, I had to learn, via philosophical triage, what I missed in order to complete a doctorate in theology at both esteemed Roman Pontifical institutions.

After the doctoral studies and well into my teaching, I decided to take the plunge and, with a little guidance from others who knew Saint Thomas, to study the *Summa theologiae*. Once I learned the structure of the Summa, how to read the Summa, and just how incredibly complete it is, I have to admit I have fallen in love with it. It is now the backbone of every class I teach in dogmatic theology here at the seminary.

So, then, a warning- do not let this happen to you. Learn philosophy, especially Saint Thomas Aquinas, the master of all Catholic thought, if you wish to study theology. The modern and contemporary period can only bring one so far without a firm grasp of the Catholic philosophical tradition. Philosophy does not teach us what to think, but rather how to think. And, as the old axiom goes, bad theology stems from bad philosophy. Msgr. Oxley's book can lead all of us to appreciate just a little bit more the great Catholic philosophical tradition and the place that it holds in expressing the perennial truth of the Catholic faith.

Rev. John P. Cush, STD
Professor of Dogmatic and Fundamental Theology
Saint Joseph's Seminary and College (Dunwoodie),
Yonkers, New York
January 13, 2026
Optional Memorial of Saint Hilary of Poitiers

# PREFACE

The title of the work is "The Sacramentality of Personhood." Famously, *Lumen Gentium*, the Dogmatic Constitution on the Church from the Second Vatican Council described the Church as the "Universal Sacrament of Salvation."[1] That is, the Church is both the universal sign and instrument of salvation. We find this teaching of the Church illumined according to the teaching of Pope Pius XII in his Encyclical *Mystici Corporis* (1943), wherein he taught that the "whole spirit" is in "each of the members" of the Church.[2] This suggest, that while the entire Church is the Universal Sacrament of Salvation, it seems that there is a way in which each member is also a sacrament of salvation. This is what drives the title and purpose of this project. The individual human person is a kind of sacrament, that is a sign and instrument. But we believe that this truth has not been supported by an appropriate metaphysics. This is the humble search of this project which has inexorably pushed us deeper into this teaching and its illumination for personhood in the context of sacramentality and the Catholic Faith. We hope to study this truth of personhood in light of a proposed metaphysics that would explain such a reality.

In the same manner that the whole spirit dwells in the whole Church, so the "whole spirit" is fully within each PERSON within the Church. Each person within the Church is thus understood as a

---

[1] *Lumen Gentium*, Dogmatic Constitution on the Church, Second Vatican Council, 1964, article 48.

[2] PIUS XII, *Mystici Corporis*, Encyclical (1943), #57, DS 3808, as found in the Catechism of the Catholic Church, #797.

WHOLE part of the Church. Could we not also apply this Catholic principle in a natural manner with regard to the political community of persons? May we conclude based on this theological reality, that indeed, by analogy, every person in society may be reverenced as a "whole" and that every person in society, by analogy with this theological truth, may be regarded as a "whole" among "wholes?"

Our first project, *Communio: A Comparison of the Second Vatican Council and John Zizioulas*, (2006) took a deeper dive in the search for personhood in the only place that the person may be found, which is in communion with others. An analysis of the term communion as found in the Dogmatic Constitution of the Church, *Lumen Gentium* (1964), and the Decree on Ecumenism, *Unitatis redintegratio* (1964), set us on a semantic adventure as to how this originally Greek term was applied in such a variety of ways theologically at the Second Vatican Council. Communion seemed to identify a destination for the Council Fathers, a place where persons were destined to be fulfilled and meet each other. The term opened us, in all of its equivocal splendor, to reach deeper and deeper into its theological application for persons in the Church, and for ecclesiology as a whole. Furthermore, it opened for us the Eastern lung of the Church, which through the brilliance of the rather contemporary 20th Century Greek Orthodox theologian Metropolitan John Zizioulas of Pergamon (1931-2023), personhood was applied as a primary theological category.

Our second project, *Personhood and Communion: A Critical Application of Relational Ontology in Ecclesiology,* (2009) sought to engage the influential Greek Orthodox Zizioulas with influential elements in contemporary North American Catholic ecclesiology. We found that theology, particularly in the discipline of ecclesiology, after the Second Vatican Council, tended much toward the ideological and the overly historical because it lacked an appropriate ontological methodology. Here the Holy Spirit led us to see the value in communion, and we permitted the concept of communion to take us deeper and deeper into the Trinity so as to find a true ontology that would lead the Church into her Trinitarian reality. Instead of retreating from the concept of communion out of fear, and out of the ambiguity of a polyvalent and equivocal use, we simply pushed further and further into a deeper discovery. Now reflecting back on that project, it is evident that the search for a true understanding of communion was intrinsically related to the implacable search for personhood. It turns out that both these realities would ultimately be rendered undefinable, but perennially of the utmost necessity, nevertheless, in any philosophical or theological endeavor. Furthermore, if both these realities were to be necessary for a worthy theological project, they must be discussed and understood in an ontological manner, so as to avoid the problem of the limitations of the merely historical, horizontal, functional, and ideological; the traps of modern ecclesiology.

Our third project, *Theology as Prayer: A Primer for the Diocesan Priest*, (2022) was with the then Academic Dean of the Pontifical North American College in Rome Italy, Reverend John P. Cush, who generously has provided the Foreword. We joined Father Cush so as to seek a practical and lived experience of applied meditative prayer to theological texts. Instead of writing about how a person is called to be immersed in theology, we knew, like the great Soren Kierkegaard, that it was now the time not to write about a concept theoretically, but to immerse ourselves within it and live it morally and spiritually. It was a novel contribution insofar as it applied the practice of *lectio divina* to theology. Here we saw how a person receives a theological text and integrates it into their personhood by taking it to mediative and contemplative prayer. It was a small contribution to manifest how the intellectual life is not to be divorced from the spiritual, human and pastoral life of the priest but is to be integrated in the Holy Eucharist, in this instance in the context of prayer before the Blessed Sacrament.

This now our fourth project, *The Sacramentality of Personhood: A Philosophical Thirst Meets Theology* (2025), was inspired by the political philosopher David Walsh, a Professor of Politics at the Catholic University of American in Washington, D.C. After studying under his mentorship as an undergraduate of the same university, we later in life became reunited with his books that had been subsequently published in the years thereafter by Professor Brendan Purcell, an Adjunct Professor in the School of Philosophy at Notre Dame University in Sydney. The dinner conversation plunged us deeply into Walsh's books, and it was there we discovered that he was finishing every thought for which we had been searching in our second project. A personal informal exchange with Professor Walsh affirmed his esteem for Balthasar and Jerome Santamaria, who had recently written a doctoral dissertation in Rome uniting Walsh and Balthasar, thus linking the search for personhood in philosophy with the same search in theology. We were then compelled to try our own small attempt to reach even more broadly and interface Walsh with a few more theologians. This small book is hopefully just a small step to unite the spiritual brilliance of Professor Walsh more with the discipline of theology. Ratzinger, Zizioulas, Maximus the Confessor and Professor John Betz are preludes in this project to serve this end.

In March of 2023 a Symposium was held at the Catholic University of American to honor the political thought of David Walsh. Emerging out of this conference is a book of essays in his honor edited by Thomas Holman and Richard Avramenko. The book was entitled *Personalism for the Twenty-First Century*. In the Preface to this anthology, Walsh describes the reciprocal gift that he has received from his students over his years of teaching as a "laboratory of thought," and as "the common political life." Walsh has not "applied" ideas to the real world, but on the contrary, has "discovered them within the dialogical process by which the world itself is constituted."[3] Philosopher James Greenaway of Saint Mary's University in San Antonio, Texas, as a result of his reflection on the work of David Walsh, suggests the sacramentality of the person as the way forward. It was Greenaway's suggestion of sacramentality that inspired the title of this project. Greenaway observes that in every encounter between persons "there is something sacred at stake."[4] "The seven sacraments of Eastern and Western Christian *ecclesia* can each be considered a heightening of the general sacramentality that pertains to the mystery of existence itself."[5] Greenaway proposes that Walsh brings out this character of "sacramentality" in personhood and suggests that, while Walsh does not use the term, it is

[3] T. HOLMAN and R. AVRAMENKO, *Personalism for the Twenty-First Century: Essays in Honor of David Walsh*, Lexington Books, 2025, viii.

[4] Ibid., J. GREENAWAY, "Luminosity Before Theory: Walsh on the Transcendence of the Person", 101.

[5] Ibid.

nevertheless a "fitting term" that is "centered on the person" whose being is the being of "transcendence in immanence, and whose essence is the essence of sacredness in the profane."[6] Greenaway argues that "sacramentality" retains the meaning of the theoretical tension of existence, which the German-American philosopher Eric Voegelin (1901-1985) used to apply the philosophical term "metaxy," originally Platonic,[7] in his own political philosophy. James Greenaway states that this concept of *metaxy*, this *in-betweenness*, as found in Plato and Voegelin, is recast in Walsh as the mystery "glimpsed in the face of the person."[8] This philosophical term, used theologically and politically, will serve to bridge the metaphysical difference between the divine and human in our project.

Finally, it is hoped that this our fourth project will be used as a secondary source for courses in undergraduate modern philosophy at a Catholic University, or even more appropriately for seminarians in the Discipleship Stage of Priestly Formation, wherein the Catholic Church desires philosophical studies to assist the seminarian in a deepened relationship with Jesus Christ. Studying modern philosophy systematically and rigorously, as the Church desires, should not preclude the content from assisting in relationality with Jesus, but rather contribute spiritually to it. Our priestly ministry in seminary formation for twelve years as an Assistant Professor, Vice-Rector,

---

[6] Ibid.

[7] See J. GREENAWAY, "Luminosity Before Theory: Walsh on the Transcendence of the Person," in *Personalism for the Twenty First Century: Essays in Honor of David Walsh*, where Greenaway notes that Voegelin borrows the term *metaxy*, meaning the in-betweenness of the infinite and the finite, from Plato and cites Plato's *Symposium*, 202-204.

[8] Ibid.

and Spiritual Director have highlighted the need for a Catholic re-appropriation of modern philosophy so as to find within it the thirst for the developed theology present in the Second Vatican Council, as opposed to a negative appropriation of what seems often to be a sincere search for truth from within communities of faith. This luminous journey through the modern philosophers as led by Professor Walsh will not only assist seminarians and future Catholic philosophers with making spiritual connections that link their philosophical study with theology, but also will connect philosophy with the practical reality of the pastoral life where truth is lived and discovered in the context of the Holy Eucharist, a fellowship of persons united in the truth of the Holy Trinity. This will assist the student to appreciate more deeply the questions emerging from the cultural context, now indeed having moved from post-modern to the post-Christian, and radically secularized world within which we find ourselves today. Seen now from a greater historical distance, we perhaps have the great opportunity to no longer look at modern philosophy as a problem to fix, but as inchoately containing answers to a question we have never allowed ourselves to ask.

Our project here is thus to provide the foundation for a renewed metaphysic to emerge rooted in the truth of personhood, particularly the eternal personhood of the Second Person of the Holy Trinity, Jesus Christ. We do not seek to replace the metaphysics of the great Scholastic Fathers, but to allow it to be informed by the ontology of personhood, which we argue is of greater philosophical value than substance. In his Encyclical *Aeterni Patris* (1879), Pope Leo XIII (1810-1903) sought to restore Christian Philosophy in his time under the primacy of the great Scholastic Doctor of the Church Saint

Thomas Aquinas (+1274), whom he saw as a revitalizer and unifier of philosophical training as an antidote to the enemies of the Catholic Faith.[9]

While Pope Leo XIII called for an increase in the study of Saint Thomas Aquinas, he did it in a manner that leaves openness to other philosophical schools and further philosophical development. Luke Arredondo astutely observes that "Leo recommends the study of Aquinas not as an answer to every problem, but as a way of recovering Saint Thomas's method, and his balance between the function of human reason and Divine Revelation."[10] One may observe in this emphasis on method, that, at the time, Pope Leo was rather prescient as he observed in this encyclical how deeply the Scholastic Fathers knew not only philosophy but also the truths of the natural order by stating that the same Fathers "were never so wholly rapt in the study of philosophy as not to give large attention to the knowledge of natural things; and indeed, the number of their sayings and writings on these subjects, which recent professors approve of and admit to harmonize with truth, is by no means small."[11]

On the way we will discover that the search begins with one's own experience of being drawn into communion with the other for fulfillment. We will refer to this concept as "the ethical." For example, in the experience of dialogical reciprocity (that is, in the experience of one's discovering of the truth through conversing with the

[9] L. ARREDONDO, "LEO XIII Beyond Rerum Novarum", in Church Life Journal, McGrath Institute for Church Life, University of Notre Dame, July 25, 2025.

[10] Ibid.

[11] LEO XIII, *Aeterni Patris*, Encyclical, August 1879, #30.

other) one experiences a form of communion; but, we will see that this ethics is not enough. We will see that ethics must have a metaphysical foundation in ontology. Once ontology is attained, the ethical must grow and develop from the ontological foundation. We can therefore say with the French and Jewish philosopher Emmanuel Levinas (1906-1995) that ethics does indeed precede ontology, meaning that our experience of communion with the other always precedes our understanding of being. We then argue that from this ontological foundation, the ethical person grows and develops through grace and the process of divinization.

It is with the same spirit of the Scholastic Fathers that we proceed into the ocean of the contribution of dialogical philosophy to our understanding of theology lived today. This is especially true in light of its contribution to the theology of the Second Vatican Council, and in the Pontificate of Pope John Paul II and his openness to contribution of other philosophical traditions in his *Fides et Ratio* (1998).

# Introduction

Part One, *The State of the Question: The Dialogical Convergence of Philosophy and Theology*, of this four part essay, begins with what we perceive as the historical moment that defined the 20th Century collectively, and the universal event held by persons of good will to be the greatest tragedy of that century, the Jewish Holocaust. From this historical point of departure, we have chosen an existential point of departure so as to illumine the gravity of the genocide of persons. Here, the collective of good-willed humanity grieves a fundamental truth of the sin of one group or race of people failing to recognize and reverence the sacred presence of God in another group of people. Paradoxically, genocide carries within it the call to bring one's attention to a sacred principle, that the human person must be reverenced, their rights must be protected, never violated. Professor John Betz reminds us that the meaning of *meta* in metaphysics carries the meaning of "toward another."[1] When another is violated a metaphysical sin occurs. We thus, ironically, find the truths of metaphysics first in ethics, that is how we are obliged to respect and listen to each other. Ethics actually bears within it the deepest metaphysical and transcendent truths, and it is within ethics that we are able to find supernatural truths. It is philosophically appropriate, therefore, that our metaphysical understanding in the Church should not be divorced from ethics and life. For if it were to be divorced, there would be a prioritization of essence at the expense

---

[1] J.R. BETZ, *Christ the Logos of Creation: An Essay in Analogical Metaphysics*, Emmaus Academic, 2023, 128.

of existence in philosophy,[2] a prioritization of concepts over lived experience, with the tragedy of ideological results, such as the horror of Nazi Fascism.

We thus begin this project in the context of ethics, where all persons of goodwill begin a philosophical search, whether known or unknown, in the context of real life. Real life, if it is received in its truth, always bears the dimensions of suffering, and the ethical obligation to receive the other. Without openness to the other, something is deficient. In fact, the deeper we receive and reverence the other, the more we become the human person whom we are called to become. For this reason, in Jewish dialogical philosophy, we find a discovery that was appreciated greatly by the Swiss theologian Hans Urs Von Balthasar (Part One, Chapter One) and Joseph Ratzinger (Part One, Chapter Two). We have also found this discovery of receptivity and relation in the very structural dynamic of theology itself. We want to state that receptivity, both to God and to the other person, is a pathway to the truth of God. The Dogmatic Constitution on the Church, *Dei Verbum*, of the Second Vatican Council captures this receptivity and dialogue between God and the person in the context of Revelation, which requires the theological understanding of reception as essential to describing Revelation itself. This opens up new dimensions in theology that more deeply appropriate otherness, relationality, and personhood. Divine Providence has enabled this great reciprocal convergence of truth in philosophy (Jewish dialogical philosophy), to bear direct similarities to the truths gleaned from a theology of Revelation (Balthasar and Ratzinger).

[2] Ibid., 134.

There is a theological culmination of these two realities converging particularly in the second chapter of *Dei Verbum.*

Part Two, *Openings: Philosophical and Theological,* in many ways mirrors Part One. Here we illustrate how this very same dynamic unfolds in the form of the political philosopher David Walsh (Part Two, Chapter Three) in his understanding of persons as the overarching category for understanding philosophy as lived politically, with deep appreciation for the modern contribution. Walsh, in the field of political philosophy, develops how the dialogical principle is so readily illumined within human relations. In Walsh we find the same truth unveiled in Jewish dialogical philosophy, yet nearly a century apart. In Walsh, we find a similar dynamic of ethics leading to theology. As Jewish dialogical philosophy led to Balthasar and Ratzinger, we have now found in David Walsh a political philosopher who leads to an emerging new theological Professor John Betz of the University of Notre Dame (Part Two, Chapter Four). Betz, like Joseph Ratzinger, desires to expand our metaphysical horizon, and actually provides the foundation for a revised metaphysic by turning to the same philosopher that Balthasar did, German Jesuit Erich Przywara (1889-1972). This will develop our understanding of Tradition as fundamentally Trinitarian, leading to the rich possibilities that this discovery lends to our developed understanding of personhood in David Walsh, and how this may be applied to the discipline of theology by way of both analogy and *metaxis.* The understanding of human personhood has the capacity to become more widely illumined and expanded in its full splendor in the light of Divine Personhood, but at the same time always retaining its difference from Divine Personhood, as the former remains undefinable as it is inserted more into the mystery of the latter.

Part Three, *Proposals: Metaphysical and Theological*, directly addresses the metaphysical question. Looking to the Seventh Century Eastern Patristic Father Saint Maximus the Confessor for a solution. While Maximus (Part Three, Chapter Five) does not provide us with a definitive metaphysic, he certainly provides us with a viable metaphysic, one that adequately captures both essence and existence without a prioritization of on over the other. Maximus creates a space for the rich development of the particular uniqueness in human personhood in a manner that the Scholastic West was not capable of doing due to the historical limits of the period. This is due, in our opinion, to the medieval political society being in the form of Kingdoms, which by their very structure, in our opinion, did not adequately give the political freedom for the human person to discover their particular uniqueness. If one had the inherent capacity for brilliant artistic creation, for example, but had been of a certain lower class, the person would not have been able to flourish in this capacity. It is not that a serf could not become a saint (surely many were), but the political structures were not in a place to permit the full breathe and depth of that sanctity to flourish. In a much earlier period in history, Saint Maximus the Confessor was able to employ a more personalist vision that was at the same time adequately metaphysical. We propose that Maximus be given a renewed metaphysical voice for our current day, certainly not replacing Saint Thomas Aquinas, but perhaps being worthily considered philosophically equal to him, or even greater.

We propose that Maximus the Confessor may be considered for philosophical study at the Discipleship Stage of Priestly Formation, along with Saint Thomas Aquinas, so that Catholic seminarians and other students of philosophy in Catholic Universities may have the advantage of learning other metaphysical systems within the Catholic Tradition that very well may more effectively assist them in their human, spiritual and pastoral lives.

As Maximus the Confessor provides us with a metaphysical foundation from an Eastern perspective, Greek Orthodox theologian Metropolitan John Zizioulas (Part Three, Chapters Six, Seven, and Eight) further opens up the dimension of personhood with his anthropology, ecclesiology, and Trinitarian theology. Serving in the Ecumenical dialogue between Christians of the East and the West, Zizioulas theologically contributes to the development of personhood. Zioualas was able to accomplish this in a modern context because of his Eastern foundation, not limited by Western metaphysics. For Maximus and Zizioulas, the theological point of departure for a theology of personhood is found in the Person of the Father and the freedom of his will to create. With Maximus and Zizioulas (a Patristic theologian and modern theologian) emerges a proposed metaphysic with ecclesiological foundations which contribute to a hopeful unity of the Christian East and West. This Eastern contribution captures the deepest theological discoveries of Balthasar and Ratzinger regarding personhood. Moving from a more person-based (rather than substance-based) metaphysic serves to open up the student of philosophy to a broader philosophical context so as to be formed philosophically in a manner that is capable of meeting the deepest existential questions of this century in the context of truth.

In Part Three, Chapter Six, Zizioulas reveals the limitations of the Western understanding of personhood as we look to new openings beyond the limitations of substance. In Part Three, Chapter Seven, we will find with Zizioulas that in other Eastern Fathers, such as Athanasius of Alexandria, substance may be found in the first instance to have a relational character. Further, in the Cappadocian Father Saint Basil the Great, we find the term *hypostasis* being used to highlight the particular characteristics of personhood. Highlighted here are movements in early Eastern Patristic theology toward illumining personhood, both divine and human. A clear example is when Basil highlights the insufficiency of the term "man" because it fails to properly individuate the person as unique and particular (such individuation is necessary in the created order). The treatment of the contribution of Zizioulas concludes in Part Three, Chapter Eight where a necessary theological epistemology is developed that is rooted in both lived experience (ethics) and communion (ontological truth), which in turn carries with it the full potential to illumine the modern political order.

In Part Four, *Conclusions: A Path Forward for Personhood,* we return again to David Walsh in Chapter Nine as we explore the full potential for the freedom of the liberal person to flourish in his or her unique particularity in the context of the truth and communion of the political community. Finally, in Chapter Ten, we develop, a greater understanding of the metaphysic of love to which the person within the ecclesial community is called with the assistance of Pope Benedict XVI and Pope Francis. In this, we find the Magisterial context of a particular and unique response to Divine Revelation.

# PART ONE

## *THE STATE OF THE QUESTION: THE DIALOGICAL CONVERGENCE OF PHILOSOPHY AND THEOLOGY*

# Chapter One

# Hans Urs Von Balthasar and Dialogical Philosophy: Convergence and Reciprocity

"No, it is something very near to you,
in your mouth and in your heart,
to do it" (Deuteronomy 30:14)

## 1.1 Existential Lessons from the Jewish Holocaust

The horror of the detention of the Jewish people between 1933 and 1945 by the Nazi regime in camps that were sites of cruelty, torture, deprivation, unchecked disease, grueling forced labor, extreme violence, and mass murder, marks the greatest apostasy against the sacramentality of personhood that the 20th century. As modern society was upended by the Holocaust, the Church had an opportunity, as it perennially does, to speak into this reality so as to give answer to the contemporary person, as epistemology was forced to grapple with this crushing reality from every angle. This event, and others like it within history, compels the manner in which we apply classical philosophy to lived realities  in order to adjust to circumstances which demand more reverence for every human person. Providentially, the death of the Son of God, Jesus Christ, on the

Cross forces the same question for classical philosophy. Will philosophy be humble enough to submit to these sacred human and divine realties that demand epistemological and metaphysical development? Will Catholic philosophy be able to respond to the great thirst of the human person to be received, affirmed, and valued in a manner that extends beyond the perceived superficial category of the emotional and into the realm of the objective, metaphysical, pastoral and truly spiritual?

Our project desires to offer the epistemology that may be constructed from a theology founded in personhood which desires to speak into such a reality. As the Church has become more accustomed to speaking into questions posed by the contemporary person, our project is to further assist in providing the epistemological pathways for this dynamic to be metaphysically substantiated. Such a tragedy that effects all of humanity due to this horror, calls for the sacramentality of personhood, so as to both assist in avoiding such ideological evils from occurring again, as well as to provide hope for persons who are immersed in such evils in the various forms within which it manifests itself in the current day.

Viktor E. Frankl, a survivor of the Nazi camps, recalls love as being the motivating factor for survival against these evils, with love propelling the human spirit to courage and dignity in the face of suffering. His *Man's Search for Meaning* (1959) recalls the brutal reality of the captors depriving the imprisoned of any form of human dignity, portraying the luminosity of the human person maintaining dignity in the face of these abominable sins by maintaining the great human choice for the inner freedom to choose an attitude of gratitude, humor, hope and purpose that could not be taken away from the captors. It was in this great human choice, in the face of the highest form of tyrannical ideology against personhood that the century had known, that the Nazi guards actually became the ones who were spiritually and humanly shackled in the face of this great capacity of human personhood overcoming the greatest of evils.[1] Despite their captivity, the great drama unfolded in the context of the affective countenance and disposition of charity and virtue embraced by the prisoners who chose love, despite their extreme and despairing circumstances. In any and every instance of similar responses in human history to direct sins against personhood, the response of love in the face of such evil captures and moves human hearts to the truth of love.

## 1.2 The Emergence of Dialogical Philosophy

It is prior to and during this time, providentially, we argue, that dialogical philosophy arises from the authentic and lived experience of the Jewish people. From the experience of their collective suffering, a rich philosophy emerges that will light the path for all of humanity so that future generations may learn the depths of what real and authentic relationships between persons are called to be. We have found that the deepest truths expressed by the dialogical philosophers have pierced and illumined what humanity may have held prior to the Holocaust, albeit in an obscure manner.

---

[1] See V.E. FRANKL, *Man's Search for Meaning*, Beacon Press, Boston, 2006.

Our search led us to a prominent theologian of the 20th Century who deeply appreciated this philosophical movement emerging out of the depths of human experience. The captives in those camps would have experienced the presence of God through the sacramentality of the other experienced in the warmth of shared language in the form of speech and the use of the personal name to express love and affection. In such a tragic human situation, afflicted with evil, the "I" needs a "thou" so that one does not fall into despair. The felt and experienced awareness of being loved by another, providentially is the same manner in which our Father God relates to us in Jesus Christ.

We therefore begin with the twentieth century Swiss theologian Hans Urs Von Balthasar (1905-1988) in whom we have found the integration of the strongest dialogical philosophical movements of the 20th Century with Revelation. Because of the appreciation of Balthasar for the dialogical, he becomes a modern theologian who most deeply incorporates the personal in the theology of the Catholic Church in the West, with a simultaneous appreciation for the East, which is what draws our project to his thought.

Balthasar himself describes the emergence of four philosophers in the early 20th century, all isolated from and very different from each other, yet at the same time all converging on the dialogical principle, as being one of the strangest phenomena of acausal contemporaneity in the history of the intellect.[2] The four philosophers at this time whom Balthasar credits with this convergence were the

---

[2] Cf. H.U. BALTHASAR, *Theo-Drama Vol.* I: *Theological Dramatic Theory*, San Francisco, 1988, 626.

Austrian Ferdinand Ebner (1882-1931), the German Franz Rosenzweig (1886-1929), the Austrian-Israeli Martin Buber (1878-1965), and the French Gabriel Marcel (1889-1973).[3] In this chapter we will provide a brief analysis of the contribution of all four of these dialogical philosophers, emphasizing how they contribute to the work of theology. Firstly, however, it is important to observe how the recent Magisterium of the Catholic Church has developed and expanded the permission for an appreciation for the convergence between faith and reason according to the principles of *Fides et Ratio*, and for the purposes of our project for the convergence of dialogical philosophy with Revelation.

## 1.3 Ferdinand Ebner - Language

We first look at the convergence of a philosophical approach to language upon theology. During the tragic events of the First World War, the German Jewish philosopher Ferdinand Ebner (1882-1931) sought to break free from some of the limitations of German idealism by an exploration of the phenomenon of language.[4] The late and recent Professor and Dean of the Pontifical Gregorian University,

---

[3] It is worth noting that Ebner, Rosenzweig and Buber were all Jewish. Noting that the Holocaust was the most tragic event of the 20th century, and its damaging effects produced cultural wounds that that will take generations to heal, to hear from the Jewish perspective regarding relationality adds even deeper connection with suffering and reality, arguably the most authentic and real philosophical font of this epoch.

[4] Cf. J. O'DONNELL, S.J., "The Trinity as Divine Community", Gregorianum, V. 69, 1988, 5-34.

John. O'Donnell, S.J., a scholar of Balthasar, offered some helpful observations on the contribution of Ebner's philosophy. O'Donnell attributes Ebner with the insight that the whole of the modern philosophical tradition represents the philosophy of the *ego* locked in upon itself.[5] While this round dismissal of modern philosophy is certainly not embraced in this project, we do concur that this period of philosophy had its limitations, such as the common rejection of the theological truth of Original Sin. Rejecting an isolated approach to truth, nevertheless, O'Donnell observed that Ebner approached language in a manner that regarded it as both a gift and a mystery,[6] which makes it rather unique with regard to its modern philosophical contribution.

As human beings, we have a need to communicate and express ourselves to others. Each human person is complex. Ebner understood well the uniqueness and complexity of the human person, as Balthasar credits him with the discovery that the human person is an "absolute unique instance."[7] One understands this quickly when one desires to communicate an idea, and the idea is neither understood, nor received, introducing a certain negative experience of frustration and emptiness immediately following on the part of the

---

[5] J. O'DONNELL, S.J., 11. Here O'Donnell describes the shift from the individualism of German idealism to a dialogical philosophy well. Referring to the individualism of Hegel, O'Donnell states that in this model the other's being is functional. The other exists to mediate my self-consciousness. The movement is always back to the I, and so Hegel presents a subtle form of individualism. Our project on the other hand, will focus more on the positive contribution of Hegel through the philosophy of David Walsh.

[6] Ibid., 12.

[7] H.U. BALTHASAR, *Theo-Drama*, Vol. 1, 645.

giver. When we are understood, such as when an idea that we desire to communicate is received, one experiences the delight of being understood, welcomed, and accepted. This dynamic is a significant existential reality that determines a significant part of the daily contentment of the modern and emotionally mature, healthy adult.

### 1.3.1 Pastoral Illustration of Ebner's Discovery

A Pastor of twenty-seven years has arrived at a new and large suburban parish. He presents himself for the first time to the parents of children preparing for the sacraments. With his pastoral remarks, he is misunderstood, despite his good and pure intentions. His remarks were made to parents of children who bring their children on a weekday evening to faith formation classes, but do not regularly attend Sunday Mass, and so did not know the Pastor well. To some of the parents, the words that the Pastor chose regarding a challenge to a greater practice of the faith were deemed offensive, and the Pastor was left misunderstood. When the Pastor used the language that he chose to communicate, he was speaking from his whole person, as faith touches the deepest level of our being. Language is therefore given and received in the context of the other, to some challenging words are deemed offensive, to others encouraging, yet the reception of the language will determine how the Pastor adjusts his language the next time that he speaks to the same group. Language is therefore a mysterious medium that so often needs to be adjusted and discerned to reach the receiver appropriately and effectively.

### 1.3.2 Ebner - Language as Gift and Mystery

Language, therefore, is the gift that enables persons to express themselves to others. Language in itself, as it requires both a giver and a receiver, as well as comprehension, illustrates clearly, from a phenomenal perspective, that as an I, I am in need of the other. Essentially, O'Donnell observed in his observations on Ebner, that I have need of the other in order to fully be myself. For if I did not have the gift of language, it would be much more difficult for me to be understood and received. Furthermore, in order to communicate, both persons rely upon the transcendental objectivity of language as a gift given to express themselves to one another. Thus, language is a gift and ultimately both objective and subjective.[8] Thus, Ebner sees correspondence between the use of the human word and the divine Word.[9]

It is therefore only as humans are addressed by the "eternal thou" that they are able to enter into the depth of communication that they desire with other human beings. While Ebner was purely a philosopher, in his project, we see, with Balthasar's help, that theology is needed in order to carry the seeds of truth within the project

[8] Ibid., 12.

[9] Cf. F. EBNER, *Parola e Amore*, 58 *Dal Di*ario 1916/1917, *Aforismi* 1931, Milan 1983. "The word is the mediator between the I and the you. The full and complete reality of the I is man. But, the true and actual you is God. This is found in the Prologue of the Gospel of John. The word was generated by the Spirit. And this therefore is the true origin of language: the spirit of God that spoke to man, and then man likewise became aware of his I. It is man that then spoke to the spirit of God, and therefore found the true you that corresponds to his I." (*translation ours*).

of dialogical philosophy. While recognizing the need for theology to complete the thought of Ebner, one also sees the need for theology to shed light on the natural phenomenon of language.

## 1.4 Franz Rosenzweig - The Personal Name

The next instance is the philosophical convergence of the personal name upon theology. When someone uses our personal name in addressing us, it is met with an experience of being affirmed, through particular language, providing the other with a sense of acceptance. The use of a name seems to change everything interpersonally for the better. The Jewish philosopher Franz Rosenzweig (1886-1929), in his, *The Star of Redemption* gives a philosophical value to the personal name. Particularly, Rosenzweig's description of the "I" and the "Thou," between Adam and God in the Garden of Eden, captures Balthasar's attention.[10] When God asks Adam "Where are you?" Adam first hides from the question, but then comes the vocative, or the summons, and Adam is thus denied any means of an escape route, because of the fact that there is a movement from the objective to the personal.[11]

This text contributes an illustrative narrative regarding the gift of the name in the above mentioned dialogue:

> The indefinite Thou was merely deictic: the woman, the serpent. Its place is taken by the vocative, the direct address, and man is cut

[10] H.U. BALTHASAR, Theo Drama, Vol. 1, p. 639.

[11] Cf. GENESIS 3: 9-11.

off from every retreat into hypostatization. The general concept of man can take refuge behind the woman or the serpent. Instead of this the call goes out to what cannot flee, to the utterly particular, to the nonconceptual, to something that transcends the sphere of influence of both the definite and indefinite articles, a sphere which embraces all things if only as objects of a universal. To God's 'Where are you?' The man has still kept silence and blocked the Self. Now, called by his name, twice, in a supreme definiteness that could not be heard, now he answers, all unlocked, all spread apart, all ready, all soul: 'Here I am.'[12]

### 1.4.1 Pastoral Illustration of Rosenzweig Discovery

When the Pastor knows the name of a person, and addresses them by name, it is as if something awakens within the person receiving the greeting. It is something similar to the awakening of Sleeping Beauty as the person awakens, because of the words of affirmation that are spoken over them, which are particular and unique to the person. The mystery becomes even greater as the awareness of the person on the part of the giver grows from this initial foundation of the name being spoken, as a relationship of mutual sharing grows and develops over time.

### 1.4.2 Rosenzweig - Naming as Being Known by God

It is here that Balthasar credits Rosenzweig with emphasizing the philosophical value of the unique name, which is how the individual

---

[12] F. ROZENZWEIG, *The Star of Redemption*, 1971, 175-176.

is principally known and addressed by God. In fact, Balthasar describes this name as the individual's perfect definition as assigned by God.[13] The personal name, he states is, "not a name personally adopted by someone of his own volition, but the name which God himself created for him; it is only personal to him because it is created as such by the Creator."[14]

One is able to see, therefore, the depth of the phenomenon of person in both Ebner and Rosenzweig. Most notably, perhaps, from these two we have a philosophy with tremendous theological import. Appreciating the divine origin of both language and name for the purpose of who the human person truly is, and is called to be, with relationship to the Holy Trinity, is of tremendous value for both philosophy and theology.

## 1.5 Martin Buber - The "I" and the "Thou"

The third instance, and perhaps the most notable from this school of dialogical philosophy is the convergence of the Jewish philosopher Martin Buber (1878-1965) upon the theological. In his seminal work, the *I and the Thou*, Buber captures the thrust of his

---

[13] Cf. H.U. BALTHASAR, *Theo-Drama*, V. I, 645. See also R. SOKOLOWSKI, *Presence and Absence: A Philosophical Investigation of Language and Being*, Bloomington, IN, 1978, 28-29 for a perspective on how naming brings about a new excellence in things (in their absence), their truthfulness. Naming, he states, makes the goodness of a thing become known. See also H. ALFONSO S.J., *Discovering your Personal Vocation: The Search for Meaning through the Spiritual Exercises*, Paulist Press, 2001.

[14] Ibid., 639.

philosophical contribution and truly synthesizes the central tenants of his dialogical philosophy.[15] Implicit within the title of the *I and the Thou* is the *a priori* recognition of the Thou. Buber states that "Egos appear by setting themselves apart from other egos. Persons appear by entering into relation with other persons."[16] Balthasar adds that for the "I" to truly be a person, there must be a "Thou."[17] Buber philosophically introduces the necessity of the other. He therefore laments the type of meeting that is impersonal, objective, and derivative, labelling it *Erfahrung*. Such an experience, O'Donnell accurately states, would limit experience to the one who experiences, without any regard for the Thou.[18] The type of meeting that Buber desires is personal, immediate and underivable, *Begenung*. Buber illustrates the difference between the two types of meetings in the following manner:

> Once the sentence 'I see the tree' has been pronounced in such a way that it no longer relates a relation between a

---

[15] Cf. J.R. CHAPEL, *Why Confess Our Sins Out Loud? An Analysis Based on the Dialogical Philosophy of Ferdinand Ebner in light of the Philosophy of Language and the Symbolic Sacramentology of Louis-Marie Chauvet*, Rome, Italy, 1999, 19. See also J. O'DONNELL, S.J., *The Trinity as Divine Community*, as he notes that there was a significant shift between the early writings of Buber, and the great turn which Buber made with the publication of the *I and the Thou.* O'Donnell states that the early Buber, while emphasizing the "I," the otherness of the other was lacking, along with the transcendence of the "Thou", 13.

[16] M. BUBER, *I and Thou*, Touchstone, 1970, 112.

[17] Cf. H.U. BALTHASAR, *Theo-Drama*, Vol 1, p.628.

[18] Cf. J. O'DONNELL, S.J, *Trinity as Divine Community*, 14.

> human I and a tree You but the perception of the tree object by the human consciousness, it has erected the crucial barrier between subject and object; the basic word I-It, the word of separation, has been spoken.[19]

### 1.5.1 Pastoral Illustration of Buber's Philosophy

A poor person shabbily dressed whom the Pastor of an affluent parish has never seen before enters unexpectedly into the church and meets the priest in the vestibule before Mass. The Pastor is morally, ethically and ontologically bound to receive the stranger in love, anything less would be unacceptable to any person of good will. Furthermore, the mandatory meeting must be personal, immediate and underivable (*Begenung*). If the meeting between the priest and the stranger were impersonal, overly objective or derivative (*Erfahrung*), the meeting would fall into isolation and into the category of nothingness. The priest is pastorally obliged to receive the other before he evaluates the other. With this *datum* accepted, the other, the "Thou," is metaphysically and ontologically constitutive of my "I." The love of the stranger demanded in this situation, prior to even knowing the stranger, makes a strong argument for the primacy of love over knowledge in epistemology. In fact, the illustration proves that love determines being. If the "thou" is *a priori* ontological to my "I," must it not follow that love precedes knowledge?

---

[19] M. BUBER, *I and Thou*, 74-75.

### 1.5.2 Buber - The Dialogical as filled with Theological Light

Like Ebner, Buber perceives the eternal Thou. Although it is not developed in his philosophy, the seed is there for the divine to be fully included. Balthasar understands Buber's I and Thou to represent a special place in the transition to a theology of dialogics. Balthasar describes it as progressively filled with theological light, although it never becomes clear, he states, what kind of theology it is- and to what extent it implies a biblical faith or a belief in a universal humanity.[20] One finds in Buber a power, or a transcendental grace, that enables a true encounter to unfold. Thus, something transcendent and spiritual is operative.[21] Balthasar finds in Buber a sober grasp of the finitude of and inherent disappointment in every relationship between human beings; manifested in the presence of the eternal Thou.[22] Both the eternal Thou and the sense of mystery are found in Buber. For example, for Buber, the human I in relationship to the Thou, however beneficial the understanding may be for understanding human relationships, is not complete unless it is understood in relationship to the eternal Thou. Silence is the ultimate goal of such an encounter. For he states that "Only silence before the Thou-silence of all tongues, silent patience in the undivided word that

---

[20] H.U., BALTHASAR, *Theo-Drama*, V: *The Last Act*, San Francisco, 1988, 632.

[21] Cf. J. O'DONNELL, S.J., *The Trinity as Divine Community*, 15. Here O'Donnell states that Buber provides yet another prelude to the theological contribution of understanding God as a communion of persons.

[22] H.U. BALTHASAR, *Theo Drama*, V. 1, 629.

precedes the formed and vocal responses – leaves the Thou free."[23] Again, if encounter leads us into silence, then encounter has led us into God's contemplative silence.

## 1.6 Marcel - The Existential Appreciation Meets Theology

Finally, we reach the existential appreciation of philosophy in theology. Neither the influence of the German Martin Heidegger (1889-1976) nor the Frenchman Jean-Paul Sartre (1905-1980) can be underestimated when considering their impact on Western philosophy. Heidegger gives an existentialist interpretation of phenomenology, and Sarte gives an atheistic interpretation of phenomenology. Heidegger understood well the stark phenomenon of the intersubjectivity amongst persons that define a being unto death, while Sartre takes an isolated position against otherness, as he understands the other to be his original sin. Heidegger justly asks the question of how one finds meaning in one's existence if existence is marked in the end only by death. Sartre grappled with the problem of death more darkly than Heidegger by asking the question of how one may understand the other as other in this tragic circumstance of being condemned to death that we find ourselves within. In Sartre's attempt for a solution, only in the act of choosing is he able to find something to protect the integrity of the freedom of the person. Both Heidegger and Sartre are searching for an ontology that leads

[23] M. BUBER, *I and Thou*, 75.

beyond death and both of these philosophers understand that one's existence is always marked by relationship with the other.

The Frenchman Gabriel Marcel (1889-1973) is among the first Catholic theologians to adequately respond to these questions. Marcel understood that Sartre's thought, best understood as viewing the world simply from the terrace of a café, as being built around individualism, keeping the other always in isolation, and as an adversary.[24] In response to Sartre, whose thought he described as *eidolocentric,*[25] he suggests the metaphysic of the gift, which is no less than the gift of presence. Marcel gives credit to both Ebner and Buber with this discovery, seeing a convergence in his own metaphysical reflections with their philosophy. This convergence occurs particularly in his personal reflections on his acceptance of the other not as an object, but as subject.[26] Marcel labels this kind of freedom that Sartre describes as freedom-as-choice, a fatal error he says, because in it being is equivalent to doing, reduced to an organized unit of behaviors and comportments. Marcel is acutely aware of the deep trends within modernism, where the human person falls into a functionalist or materialist mentality, which is individualistic at its root, and with which the sense of the being of the person is lacking.[27]

---

[24] Cf. G. MARCEL, *The Philosophy of Existentialism*, New York, 1962, , 259.

[25] Ibid., 56.

[26] Cf. G. MARCEL, *The Existential Background of Human Dignity*, Harvard, 1963, 41.

[27] Cf. G. MARCEL, *The Philosophy of Existentialism*, 9,

Marcel therefore properly engages Sartre around the questions of freedom and being.[28]

### 1.6.1 MARCEL - TRACES OF A METAPHYSIC

For Marcel, this metaphysical approach to being-as-gift has much to do with the human interior affective disposition that accepts the presence of the other. Marcel speaks metaphysically about this interior movement, which provides the foundation for an adequate Catholic response to the question posed by the philosophy of existentialism. He states that when someone, some other, comes into our lives, an influx may occur that conveys an interior accretion, an accretion from within, that comes into being as soon as presence is effective.[29] As persons dispose themselves for the influx, others are no longer regarded as objects, and so the soul can no longer think in terms of *cases*; as in its eyes there are no *cases* at all.[30] For Marcel, the most legitimate use of the soul's freedom is the knowledge that it does not belong to itself.[31] He considers that the ontology of the person, the freedom of the person, is so bound with the other that the acceptance of the other as gift leads to an actual *accretion in* being.

---

[28] Cf. G. MARCEL, *The Philosophy of Existence*, 86. See also J. RATZINGER, *Truth and Freedom,* Communio (US) 25, Spring 1996, 16-35. Here Ratzinger comments on Sartre as a man who condemns humans to freedom. He states that Sartre lacks the concept of truth in his understanding of freedom. It is anarchic freedom, Ratzinger states, that makes humans pointless beings.

[29] Cf. G. MARCEL *The Philosophy of Existentialism*, 38.

[30] G. MARCEL, *The Philosophy of Existentialism*, 85.

[31] Ibid.

Those, therefore, who do not accept their entire life as a gift are doomed to see themselves like the men of Heidegger and Sartre, as mere victims of a cosmic catastrophe flowing into an alien universe bound by nothing.[32] People actually become more of who they are called to be by giving themselves to the other. For persons to give themselves to the other, they must be able to receive the other, and for Sartre, to receive is incompatible with being free.[33]

## 1.7 Balthasar: The Meeting of Modern Dialogical Philosophy with Theology

It is in Balthasar that we can find a convergence of the above-mentioned points. The existential crisis of the Holocaust as well as the discoveries of these modern philosophers find convergence in the theology of Balthasar. While our current period of time is certainly beyond the modern period of time to which Balthasar was engaging with the dialogical philosophy of the 20th century, his work is no less relevant for today. While we have since passed from a post-modern period into a post-Christian, post-truth, or secular period, the human person, when grappling with the questions of truth and existence, finds his or herself in no less of an isolated situation, or perhaps because of the tyranny of technology, social media, and the rise of new forms of ideological tyranny, the human person finds his or her self in an even more isolated situation today than ever before. With the increasing rates of suicide, chemical dependency and mass

---

[32] Ibid., 102

[33] Ibid., 82.

shootings in our American culture, there needs to be a clarion call in the theological world to respond to these cries of the human heart for love and communion by presenting anew *interpersonal communion*, in all of its philosophical splendor, as the highest form of a rational response to beauty, goodness and truth.

This convergence found in Balthasar is substantiated and legitimized as a theological pursuit by recent Magisterial texts, most notably, *Fides et Ratio*.

### 1.7.1 *Fides et Ratio* – Person as Point of Departure

It would be difficult to argue against the fact that the movement toward a more relational notion of the person in contemporary thought may indeed be regarded as a deeper convergence with Trinitarian reality.[34] The Encyclical of Pope Saint John Paul II (1920-2005), *Fides et Ratio* (1998), epistemologically validates the two ways of coming to know God: the first being through a faith that seeks to understand more, and the second through an understanding that leads to faith.[35] While the method of Balthasar is more defined by the former, there is certainly a deep appreciation also of the latter within his theology.[36] Furthermore, one could argue that it is important that in this encyclical Pope Saint John Paul II places faith as

---

[34] Cf. J . S. GRABOWSKI, *Person, Substance and Relation*, Communio (US), V. 22, Spring 1995, 139-163.

[35] Cf. JOHN PAUL II, *Fides et Ratio*, Encyclical. (1998) Chapter II, *Credum et intellegam* and Chapter III, *Intellego ut credam*.

[36] See L. CHAPP, *Who is the Church?* "The Personalistic Categories of Balthasar's Ecclesiology", in Communio (US) V. 23 (1996), 322-338.

a way of knowing *first*, as this places Revelation as essentially the font of all knowledge, truly its rightful place, regardless of the manner by which one may arrive.

Because of this, all knowledge certainly must be rooted in the Revelation of God as Triune; but, on the other hand, the Holy Trinity is also, we argue, analogically seen in the natural order through persons in communion with each other. Personhood glimpsed in nature thus leads to ultimate truths. The elements of personhood, along with personhood itself, in nature, arrive at God through the truth of the experience of communion with other persons, as John Paul II understood communion with others to be the highest natural truth in this encyclical.

We, therefore, propose a hybrid of these two epistemological approaches presented in *Fides et Ratio*. We propose with Pope John Paul II that arriving at belief in God through the truth of communion with others is the highest natural truth, which is why this great philosopher who became Pope understood the truth of the communion of persons so prominently as the culmination of natural knowledge.[37] The great Polish Pope speaks of the human person as "not made to live alone," and that in *believing* we "entrust ourselves to the knowledge acquired by other people." The Pope teaches that "what is sought is the truth of the person, what the person is and what the person reveals from deep within. Human perfection, then, consists not simply in acquiring an abstract knowledge of the truth,

---

[37] JOHN PAUL II, *Fides et Ratio,* Encyclical , #31-37, Chapter Three. (*intellego ut credam*).

but in a dynamic relationship of faithful self-giving with others."[38] We argue that this teaching establishes interpersonal communion as being the highest form of reason which leads to faith. Furthermore, this claim is substantially founded in the Second Vatican Council's Pastoral Constitution on the Church in the Modern World, *Gaudium et Spes*, Article 24, which concludes that "man cannot fully find himself except through a sincere gift of himself."[39]

This philosophical and epistemological proposal thrusts personhood into the forefront of philosophical thought. While it has often been assumed that the epistemological point of departure must be either *belief seeking understanding* (as seen in chapter two of *Fides et Ratio*) or *understanding seeking belief* (as seen in chapter three of *Fides et Ratio*), personhood proves to be a common point of departure. With this principle established, it is a given that personhood itself is both divine and human, and so we are placed before a great mystery of divine and human personhood in our search for truth. Personhood precludes the necessity of describing a journey of truth by one route or another. Rather, we argue that *personhood* becomes a *hybrid*, an actual *confluence* to make a *common point* of epistemological departure. As stated earlier, all knowledge must be rooted in the Holy Trinity, but is also analogically seen in the natural order

---

[38] Ibid., #32.

[39] GAUDIUM ET SPES, Pastoral Constitution on the Church in the Modern World, Second Vatican Council,1965, #24. Auxiliary Bishop of Krakow Karol Wojtyla was a *peritus* of the Second Vatican Council, attending every session, and a critical philosophical and theological expert in the drafting of this Constitution of the Church in the Modern World, which appreciated the contributions of modern philosophy.

through persons in communion with each other. Here, the person bears a likeness to God that is beyond any other created being, in a way that demands reverence before its mystery, and we thus argue the person is sacramental in its reality in the light of this great phenomenological reality.

### 1.7.2 Pastoral Illustration - The Woman at the Well

A model for this based in Divine Revelation is found in the Gospel of John chapter four, where Jesus meets the Samaritan Woman at Jacob's Well, and the first request that Jesus asks her is, "Give me a drink."[40] His mode of entry into a dialogue is to ask something from her. Jesus approaches her not in a spectacular manner surrounded by angels but more as a man who is wayfaring and thirsty. He is a man who desires to enter into a conversation, a dialogue. Does not every pastoral encounter need to be defined according to these terms? Jesus values closeness and proximity that fills his affectivity; the manner in which he looks at her, and the tone of voice that he chooses to use. All of these choices have a significant effect on the outcome of this conversation. This ordinary moment becomes grace filled in the life of the woman through the exchange of dialogue. The love of Jesus is a love that does not humiliate, but accepts us where we are, and then calls us to deeper conversion. The woman would rather hide, but Jesus gently brings her into the wellspring of his light. The woman at the well discovers her own self in the mystery

[40] THE GOSPEL OF JOHN, 4:7.

of Christ, as she arrived at this place of illumination and conversion through the divine dialogue.

### 1.7.3 *Donum Veritatis* - Discovering Oneself in the Truth

More precisely, and towards a possible way forward regarding a methodology that may employ these concepts theologically, the Congregation for the Doctrine of the Faith in its *Donum Veritatis*: *On the Ecclesial Vocation of the Theologian*, (1990) describes the work of a theologian as responding to a dynamism that is found within the faith itself.[41] Truth seeks to be "communicated" as man was created "for the perception of truth."[42] The theologian is therefore tasked with explaining the truth in a manner that is not only received by the intellect, but by the whole person. For example, if interpersonal communion is the highest form of rational response to the isolation that the human person often finds himself or herself within today, then the theologian is tasked with connecting the Trinitarian truth of Revelation with the human thirst so evident in this question. "From the depths of one's being, there is the desire for knowledge."[43] As the whole person thirsts for knowledge, it is the theologian's task therefore to connect this desire with the existential dimension of the person so that the person may "discover himself in the truth" and find their his or her salvation.[44] How may one

---

[41] DONUM VERITATIS, *Congregation for the Doctrine of the Faith*, 1990, #7.

[42] Ibid.

[43] Ibid.

[44] Ibid.

discover oneself in the truth? We emphasize here the existentially oriented word choice of the Congregation; the call is indeed to self-discovery, but in the truth. When one discovers oneself, one discovers what will illumine their particular, unique and integral humanity; the discovery does not reduce the humanity that is lived out in a particular mode of existence but only gives it eternal and ontological value. One needs another to discover oneself, as one must go out of one-self to another for this discovery, and one of the fruits of this going out of oneself is a deeper self-awareness. One cannot be self-aware in isolation, and the more deeply one enters in relationship with the other, the more self-aware one becomes.

This reality must develop into a proper ontology of otherness, and for that we must look to the East for its full flowering, because a more developed metaphysics in the West that can capture the otherness inherent in the understanding of personhood is more urgent now than ever before. Referring to *Fides et Ratio*, The First Chapter, "The Revelation of God's Wisdom," captures this porous relationship between Revelation and personhood in a section entitled "Reason before the Mystery," wherein we see:

> To assist reason in its effort to understand the mystery there are the signs which Revelation itself presents. These serve to lead the search for truth to new depths, enabling the mind in its autonomous exploration to penetrate within the mystery by use of reason's own methods, of which it is rightly jealous. Yet these signs also urge reason to look beyond their status as signs in order to grasp the deeper meaning which they bear. They contain hidden truth to which the mind is drawn

> and which it cannot ignore without destroying the very signs which it is given.[45]

The origin of all knowledge is the Triune God, and the Triune God is reflected in the mystery of human personhood. Personhood is the sign, and interpersonal communion, with all of its natural dynamics and truth bearing insight, is transcendental, and it points to the supernaturally defining reality of all interpersonal relationship, occurring eternally in the Triune God.

## 1.8 Conclusion

The call of both the philosopher and the theologian is to continue to find openings for these philosophical and theological principles which bear the presence of the spirit and reflect the Trinitarian communion. It is this communion to which we are called in order to integrate these dialogical principles more deeply in the very metaphysical and theological methodology from which we live in the Church, so as to have an even deeper anthropology of human persons illumined by Revelation.

Part Two of this project will treat more specifically opportunities for these openings in the form of the political philosopher David Walsh (Chapter Three) and the theologian Professor John Betz (Chapter Four). From there in Part Three we must turn to concrete

---

[45] JOHN PAUL II, *Fides et Ratio*, Encyclical, Pope Saint John Paul II, 1998, #13.

proposals in both Saint Maximus the Confessor (Chapter Five) and Metropolitan John Zizioulas (Chapters Six, Seven, and Eight).

We now, in Part One Chapter Two, turn to a contemporary of Balthasar, the German theologian Joseph Ratzinger (1927-2022), a co-founder with Balthasar of the *International Theological Review: Communio* (1972), and the insight, prior to the founding of this towering Post-Conciliar theological journal, with a glimpse into the same Council to which he richly theologically contributed.

# CHAPTER TWO

# JOSEPH RATZINGER AND *DEI VERBUM*: REVELATION AS DIALOGICAL

"Give me a drink" (John 4:7)

## 2.1 THE STATE OF THE QUESTION – THE FIRST VATICAN COUNCIL

The Dogmatic Constitution, *Dei Filius* (1870), of the First Vatican Council in its second chapter, which addresses Revelation, first speaks of God's Revelation through creation and then goes on to address historical Revelation.[1] This methodology is traditionally understood as the *preambula fidei*, which is recognized as natural knowledge being prior to the divine act of faith.[2] It is certainly valid, but a weakness is that it could remain at the level of the intellectual alone, without the involvement of love. For example, chapter three of *Dei Filius*, which pertains to theological faith, defines faith as the

---

[1] Cf. DEI FILIUS, First Vatican Council, in *Decrees of the Ecumenical Councils*, Vol . II, ed. N.P. Tanner S.J., 806. "The same Holy Mother Church holds and teaches that God, the source and end of all things, can be known with certainty from the things that were created through the natural light of human reason."

[2] Cf. K. RAHNER, H. VORGRIMLER, ed. *Dictionary of Theology*, Chestnut Ridge, NY, 1985, 403.

full submission of the intellect and will to God.[3] At this period in the Church's history, dogma was focused on the rational assent to propositions proposed by the Church and based primarily in a notional understanding. This method brought emphasis to the distinction between nature and grace, especially the supernatural reality of the latter, while at the same time very positively and necessarily solidified these doctrinal distinctions for the Faith.

While it is certainly necessary and helpful that we have the above distinction within the Tradition provided by the First Vatican Council, there was nevertheless the need for a further development wherein: 1) the person of the Father who gives the Revelation would be emphasized as prior to the content itself, and 2) that the act of faith would be deepened to include the more existential reality of the *whole self* being given freely to God.[4]

## 2.2 Joseph Ratzinger – A Bridge from Vatican I to Vatican II

Joseph Ratzinger (1927-2022) highlights the *status quaestionis* beginning with the earliest stage in his theological life. Ratzinger

---

[3] cf. DEI FILIUS, First Vatican Council, in *Decrees of the Ecumenical Councils,* Vol . II, ed. N.P. Tanner S.J., 807. "Since human beings are totally dependent on God as their Creator and Lord, and created reason is completely subject to uncreated truth, we are obliged to yield to God the revealer full submission of intellect and will by faith."

[4] Cf. DEI VERBUM, *Dogmatic Constitution on Divine Revelation*, Second Vatican Council, in the *Decrees of the Ecumenical Councils*, Vol. II, ed., N.P. Tanner S.J., Article 5, "Deo revelanti praestanda est oboeditio fidei, quao homo se totum libere committit."

understood how deeply the dialogical philosophy of the 20th Century, explored in Chapter One, assisted the understanding of the manner in which the Father relates to his son or daughter, and that there is a reciprocal love shared between the Divine Person of the Father, through the Son, and the human person. The dialogical structure of the philosophers, between the "I" and the "Thou," he understood as a gateway to a deeper illumination into the relationship between God and the human person, allowing personal and relational means of communicating to enter into the very structure of understanding Divine Revelation itself. Ratzinger's contribution in this way leads to an essential theological development of the Second Vatican Council. That is, he contributes to the development that understands Revelation as fundamentally dialogical, and the dialogical as only fulfilled through vulnerability and mutual sharing, wherein God speaks to the human person as a "friend."[5]

This leads to the Constitution on Divine Revelation of the Second Vatican Council, *Dei Verbum* (1965) which signified a theological development which is essential for the interpretation of the entire Council, the manner in which he understand how Divine Revelation is received by the human person. Insofar as Jesus is not created, creation bears the space for Jesus to work so that all may be made subordinate to him. The Father creates through the Eternal Word, and because of the relationship between the Father and the Son we may claim that language is founded eternally in God. When

---

[5] DEI VERBUM, *Dogmatic Constitution on Divine Revelation*, Second Vatican Council, in the *Decrees of the Ecumenical Councils*, Vol. II, ed., N.P. Tanner S.J., Article 2.

God reveals himself to Moses as "I Am" he is revealing himself as timeless and places the possibility for every encounter with Him in the eternal.

### 2.2.1 Pastoral Illustration

We recently heard from a very wise and experienced former Rector of a Seminary that he passed on to the seminarians in his care the wise axiom that "books cannot talk back to you." This Seminary Rector, far from being anti-intellectual, as he was formed in sound Thomistic philosophy, was using the example to illustrate that the pastoral life of a priest demands that the priest must enter into mutual human self-awareness to be pastorally effective, as this is essential for building trust. The most effective and deepest manner to grow in trust is through vulnerability and sharing, that which a book cannot reciprocate. If a seminarian only gleaned his knowledge from books, divorced from the reality of experience, then something would be lacking in his intellectual formation and it would not readily apply well to the pastoral life.

## 2.3 *Dei Verbum* as Theological Development

This understanding of Divine Revelation in its first instance as the desire of the Father to communicate himself in love to human persons serves as an opportunity for more deeply integrating one's intellectual life with one's spiritual life. The progression manifests the movement from more of a natural mode of discovering God, which is the method provided by *Dei Filius*, to the Constitution on

Divine Revelation, *Dei Verbum* (1965), of the Second Vatican Council. In this movement from the First Vatican Council to the Second Vatican Council we have come to appreciate a positive development towards a greater understanding of Divine Revelation as first being understood as a communion among persons; divine and human. We may similarly state that truth arises through the dialogical process. That is to say, truth is not created in the dialogical, but it emerges with clarity from there, as it also rises in the person of the believer as the believer receives Revelation. Furthermore, truth emerges in the political community from persons entering into authentic dialogue with each other.

This more personalist methodology of *Dei Verbum* opens up a door to relate to God in a theological manner that is essentially more deeply relational. A biblical foundation for this reality is found when God reveals himself to Moses in Exodus Chapter 3 in the Burning Bush, as "I Am," God reveals his name in the context of a dialogue, in a manner that is mysterious, utterly transcendent, and ineffable. It signifies a development from a period in the Church where reason needed to be reasserted (Vatican I) to a period in the Church where relationality and personhood (Vatican II) was needed as a prevailing methodology so as to emphasize the more relational dynamic of the faith. Christopher Collins, S.J. notes this movement from the more abstract and academic language to a language that is more human and personal, as being a contribution of Ratzinger to the Second Vatican Council.[6] The relational language does not contradict

---

[6] Cf. C.S. COLLINS, *The Word Made Love: The Dialogical Theology of Joseph Ratzinger*, Liturgical Press, 44.

reason, but applies reason in its own manner to accept the fundamental premise of the dialogical contribution occurring in philosophy, which is inherent in Revelation itself. This developed method is neither less doctrinal nor less reasonable; nor is it less dependent on grace. Rather, it is simply more relational and dialogical. The method mysteriously illumines doctrine through the lens of personhood, yet remains without a renewed metaphysics, which is now inherently demanded by the development.

This leads to a relationship with theology that is more integral and accessible to the lived experience of the Christian who seeks the closeness of God in the depth of one's heart, and in the trials, joys, pains and circumstances of one's daily life. *Dei Verbum* begins with the narrative of God acting in history, and then indicates in the fifth article the way in which the human person responds to this Revelation from God. The response called for is that of the whole person, *totum (*whole self), by a free inner gift of his or her self to God who reveals to the person and gives grace ("interior help") which "moves the heart" and "opens the eyes" in the obedience of faith.[7]

### 2.3.1 The History of Dei Verbum

The Dogmatic Constitution of the Second Vatican Council on Divine Revelation, *Dei Verbum*, therefore, contributes to an understanding of both *the God who reveals* and *the person who responds* to Revelation. However, the journey to this contribution of the Second

---

[7] DEI VERBUM, *Dogmatic Constitution on Divine Revelation,* Second Vatican Council, 1965, Article 5.

Vatican Council was not without arduous struggle.[8] Joseph Ratzinger, soon to be *peritus*, was asked by the Archbishop of Cologne, Cardinal Frings, to review the draft-text, *Constitutionis Dogmaticae De Fontibus*, which had been approved by Pope John XXIII on July 13, 1962. The draft-text was sent out to the members of the Council prior to discussion within the Council itself.[9] The thoughts of Joseph Ratzinger on the theological method employed in the draft-text are very helpful for understanding the categories of personhood in the context of Revelation. In his *Memoirs* Ratzinger recalls his review of the preliminary texts for Cardinal Frings:

> He now began to send me these texts regularly in order to have my criticism and suggestion for improvement. Naturally, I took exception to certain things, but I found no grounds for radical rejection of what was being proposed, such as managed to put through. It is true that the documents bore only weak traces of the biblical and patristic renewal of the last decades, so that they gave an impression of rigidity and narrowness through their excessive dependence on Scholas-

---

[8] cf. R. FISICHELLA, "Dei Verbum 1: History", in R. FISICHELLA and R. LATOURELLE eds., *Dictionary of Fundamental Theology*, New York, NY, 1994, 215-216. Cf. J. RATZINGER, *Commentary on the Documents of Vatican II*, ed., H. Vorgrimler, 159. The Preparatory Theological Commission for the document on revelation was chaired by Cardinal Ottaviani of the Holy Office, with Sebastian Tromp, Professor of Apologetics at the Pontifical Gregorian University as Secretary. Fisichella notes that it was due to the skill of Tromp in providing a draft summary that the complex subject was discussed in an organized manner.

[9] Cf. R. FISICHELLA, "Dei Verbum 1: History," 215.

tic theology. In other words, they reflected more the thought of scholars than of shepherds. But I must say that they had a solid foundation and had been carefully elaborated.[10]

The theological desires of the young Father Ratzinger were vindicated at the Council, where the draft-text prepared by the Preparatory Theological Commission was rejected.[11] Ratzinger was then added as a *peritus* to a mixed-Commission. The final text, with revisions, was officially promulgated under the Pontificate of Paul VI on November 18, 1965. Notably, the distinctions between Scripture and Tradition as independent sources[12] were removed, which emphasized that the Fathers of the Council chose not to reduce the content

---

[10] J. RATZINGER, *Milestones Memoirs* 1927-1977, San Francisco, CA, 1998. See also J. WICKS S.J, *Investigating Vatican II: It's Theological Turn and Biblical Commitment*, Washington D.C, 2018, 88: "As a matter of principle, Ratzinger stated that the council texts 'should not be treatises in a scholastic style, as if they were taken over from textbooks of theologians, but should instead speak the language of Holy Scripture and the holy Fathers of the Church". This most recent book by Fr. Wicks, S.J., a former Professor of Fundamental Theology at the Pontifical Gregorian University, is the fruit of years of theological and historical reflection on the texts of the Second Vatican Council.

[11] Cf. J. WICKS, S.J, *Investigating Vatican II*, 63-64. Ratzinger, who had produced an alternative draft text with Karl Rahner, had been giving lectures to groups of bishops. "On October 10, (1962), the day before the opening liturgy, Joseph Ratzinger spoke the German-speaking bishops on the serious problems with the draft text *The Sources of Revelation*."

[12] Cf. R. FISICHELLA, "Dei Verbum I: History", 216. Cf. J. RATZINGER, "Dogmatic Constitution on Divine Revelation: Origin and Background" in *Commentary on the Documents of Vatican II*, ed., H. Vorgrimler, ed. III, New York, NY, 1969, 159.

of Revelation to historical events alone. According to the analysis of Avery Cardinal Dulles, S.J., against such an overly historical approach to Revelation, the Fathers held that God himself in his eternal reality is the primary content or object of Revelation.[13] Ratzinger reflects in his commentary on the fruits of this return to the original sources: "The struggle over the Constitution on Revelation was undoubtedly the liberation from the narrow view and the return to what actually happens in the positive sources, before it was crystallized into doctrine, when God 'reveals' himself, and thus a re-appraisal of the whole nature and basis of Christian existence."[14] Collins observes:

> As the deliberations at the council unfolded, from Ratzinger's perspective, it became more and more clear to the fathers that they must treat the question of revelation in terms of its necessarily historical character. Consequently, as they engaged the historical character of revelation they simultaneously shaped the character of the theological reflection in the narrative of God's intersection with humanity. As a result, the language of the council and subsequently much of theological reflection became more accessible pastorally and spiritually to the people of God.[15]

---

[13] Cf. COLSON, C and NEUHAUS, R.J. eds, *Your Word is Truth: A Project of Evangelicals and Catholics Together*, Grand Rapids, MI, 2002.

[14] J. RATZINGER, "Dogmatic Constitution on Divine Revelation: Origin and Background", ed. H. Vorgrimler, 170.

[15] C.S. COLLINS, *The Word Made Love: The Dialogical Theology of Joseph Ratzinger*, 43.

Collins notes that the recognition that God has spoken to humanity in Christ as the eternal "I," and that by way of relationship with Christ we can turn and speak to God in the depths of our subjectivity, is the basis of Ratzinger's understanding of the whole of the Christian mystery, including Christology, ecclesiology and soteriology.[16] Collins continues by looking at the second doctoral work of Ratzinger, in his *Habilitationsschrift*, which interpreted Saint Bonaventure's theology of history and indeed created problems for him with regards to his understanding of human reception in the act of Revelation. German Professor Michael Schmaus believed that Ratzinger was opening a door to a "subjectivization" of Revelation and the simultaneous dismissing of Revelation's objective and eternal truth.[17] Ratzinger, in turn, deleted the allegedly "subjectivist" aspect of his analysis.[18] Collins goes on to explain that Ratzinger interprets Bonaventure's understanding of Revelation as being the *act* of revealing by God, not simply the *content* of what is ultimately revealed. Revelation is more categorized as a dynamic *unfolding event*, not as a static body of data or knowledge, giving it a narrative texture more than a propositional one, making it much more conducive to the reception of a person. Ratzinger understood that for Bonaventure "the *understanding* of Scripture was itself a gradual, progressive, historical development, which is not closed."[19]

---

[16] Ibid., 59.

[17] Ibid., 26 citing Fergus Kerr, *Twentieth Century Catholic Theologians*, Wiley-Blackwell, 2006, 185.

[18] Ibid., citing Ratzinger, *Milestones*, 108.

[19] Ibid., 27 citing Ratzinger, *Theology of History in Saint Bonaventure*, 57.

*Dei Verbum*, though promulgated under the Pontificate of Paul VI, may be considered from a doctrinal perspective the source document, or hermeneutical key, to the other documents of the Council. The Council begins and ends with the discussion of *Dei Verbum*,[20] thus providing a theological hermeneutic from which to proceed and conclude. René Latourelle likens the emergence of *Dei Verbum* to a method of approaching Revelation that is more personalist, historical and Christocentric, and less extrinsicist, temporal, and notional.[21] Joseph Ratzinger's Commentary on *Dei Verbum* describes the theological dimensions of the renewed appreciation of the relation between word and event in the structure of Revelation.[22] Ratzinger states: "The Fathers were merely concerned with overcoming neo-scholastic intellectualism, for which Revelation chiefly meant a store of mysterious supernatural teachings, which automatically reduces faith very much to an acceptance of these supernatural insights."[23]

The unique nature of this Constitution is that it begins with the personal Revelation of God and salvation in Jesus Christ, under the invitation to "friendship," a different point of departure from that of the First Vatican Council, which spoke first of God's Revelation

---

[20] Cf. R. LATOURELLE, "Dei Verbum II: Commentary" in *Commentary on the Documents of Vatican II*, ed., H. Vorgrimler, ed. III, New York, NY, 1969, 218. Here Latourelle states that "Dei Verbum was one of the first constitutions submitted for discussion, and one of the last to be voted upon."

[21] Ibid.

[22] J. RATZINGER, "Dogmatic Constitution on Divine Revelation: Origin and Background", ed. Vorgrimler, 172.

[23] Ibid.

through creation, and then of historical Revelation.[24] Thus, a hermeneutic is provided by the former through which all contemplative and personal pondering, along with the acceptance of doctrinal and dogmatic truths, may be applied; that is, through the origin of the personhood of the Father, and the fullness of his Revelation in the person of Jesus Christ,[25] and the invitation into this fellowship of friendship to which we are now invited.

The theology of Henri De Lubac, S.J., serves as a catalyst for placing the mystery of Christ in the foreground of Revelation. While conceptual expressions, along with their notions and propositions, are understood in his theology as necessary, they are nevertheless only illumined by the centrality of the mystery of Christ.[26] De Lubac recognizes that the normative truth of the mystery should govern our understanding of precise formulas, the normative truth being

---

[24] Cf. R. LATOURELLE, "Dei Verbum II: Commentary," *Dictionary*, 218.

[25] Cf. T. NEAL and J. GRESHAM, *Wonder and the Prayerful Study of Theology*, Institute for Priestly Formation, Omaha, NE, 2017. These two experienced seminary theologians introduce the seminarian to praying with the doctrine of the Church by using the Chalcedonian Creed as a doxology. The methodology of *Dei Verbum* serves to enhance this experience insofar as the seminarian is able to ponder the doctrine of the Church in relation to, and as a gift from, the person of the Father. Doctrine will then be received not only intellectually, but into the inner recesses of the heart of the seminarian, thus giving him the tools to align his hour of prayer in the presence of the Blessed Sacrament to his theological study in the classroom.

[26] Cf. R. LATOURELLE, *Theology of Revelation*, Staten Island, NY, 1966, 228.

central to the rediscovery that the mystery of the person of Christ contains the whole of Revelation and the whole of dogma.[27]

This Christocentric understanding of Revelation leaves ample space for preserving and protecting the presence of mystery in our understanding of the act of faith, which thus enables the theological virtue of faith to reach into the deeper levels of the human heart, to which conceptual answers are insufficient.[28] It becomes evident that, since this methodology is centered on the divine personhood of the Father and of Christ, it is *apophatic*. Here, the divine may never be reduced to our own concepts or formulations. With person and mystery at the forefront, we are invited to understand Revelation as a dialogical event initiated by the Father.

Article One of *Dei Verbum* begins by stating that: "The Word of God calls for *reverent* attention."[29] Reverent attention is a posture for prayer, which appreciates the Word of God as a divine gift, extending from the fullness of the love of the Father and demanding a response from the person rooted in a reverently prayerful en-

---

[27] Ibid.

[28] Ibid. See also the trilogy of books written by Fr. Donald Haggerty, an experienced seminary spiritual director on contemplative prayer for a masterful exposition of how concepts are not sufficient for the soul who grows deeper in the spiritual life (*Contemplative Provocations*, San Francisco, CA, 2013; *Contemplative Hunger*, San Francisco, CA, 2016; *Contemplative Enigmas*, San Francisco, CA, 2020).

[29] DEI VERBUM, Second Vatican Council, *Decrees of the Ecumenical Councils*, Vol. II, ed., N.P. Tanner S.J., 971; Latin original: "Dei Verbum religiose audiens et fidenter proclamans."

counter.[30] We thus posit that *lectio divina* becomes the foundation for the deepest reception of Divine Revelation, as the Dogmatic Constitution first calls the recipient to a reverent hearing and attention to the presence of God within his Word.

Article Two of the same Dogmatic Constitution further extends this invitation of the Father as it speaks of God "revealing himself" to the human person, as he "speaks to man as friends and enters into their life" so as to "invite and receive them into relationship with himself."[31] Joseph Ratzinger understands this article as being dialogical in character, particularly because of the use of the verbs indicating dialogue, such as *alloquitor* and *conservatur* .[32] Such verbs, used by the Council Fathers to describe the friendship of God with human persons, are examples of the dialogical import of Revelation in terms of the *Word*, for every word presupposes an "I" and a "Thou" and implies that the "I" intends to be understood by the "Thou".[33]

---

[30] Cf. R. LATOURELLE, "Dei Verbum II: Commentary," *Dictionary*, 218.

[31] DEI VERBUM, *Dogmatic Constitution on Divine Revelation*, Second Vatican Council, *Decrees of the Ecumenical Councils*, Vol. II, ed., N.P. Tanner S.J., 972; Latin original: "Hac itaque revelatione Deus invisibilis ex abundantia caritatis suae homines tamquam amicos alloquitor et cum eis conversatur."

[32] J. RATZINGER, "Dogmatic Constitution on Divine Revelation: Origin and Background", ed. H. Vorgrimler, 171.

[33] Cf. R. LATOURELLE, *Theology of Revelation*, 228. See also S. PIENINOT, *La Teologia Fundamentale*, Brescia, 2007, 83-84.

This understanding of *word* carries with it an existential delegation.[34]

Furthermore, as mentioned above, Article Five of *Dei Verbum*, in a development from Vatican I, describes the assent to Revelation as assent to the Revelation *God* gives,[35] placing emphasis on the person of the Father giving the Revelation (the Who) rather than simply assenting to the truth of what has been revealed by God (the what).[36] Joseph Ratzinger comments that this change of emphasis "opens up a new vista, which again in no way removes the intellectual component of faith, but understands it as a component to a wider whole."[37] It thus becomes evident that the Fathers of the Second Vatican Council desired to personalize Revelation.[38]

Thus, when God reveals, he does not reveal propositions and statements, but his very *Self* as Revelation, as he did for Moses in the Burning Bush, penetrating to the very core of humanity that was created by the same Word of God,[39] and then asks for the complete gift of the human person in return. The response of the human persons

---

[34] Cf. R. LATOURELLE, *Theology of Revelation*, 324-325. See also J. ALFARO, S.J.," Persona Y Gracia" in Gregorianum Vol. 41, Rome, 1960, 5-29.

[35] Cf. DEI VERBUM, *Decrees of the Ecumenical Councils*, Vol. II, ed., N.P. Tanner S.J., 973. Emphasis mine.

[36] J. RATZINGER, "Dogmatic Constitution on Divine Revelation: Origin and Background", ed. H. Vorgrimler, 178. Cf. DEI FILIUS, *First Vatican Council*, Vol. II, ed., N.P. Tanner S.J., 807.

[37] J. RATZINGER, "Dogmatic Constitution on Divine Revelation: Origin and Background", ed. H. Vorgrimler, 178.

[38] Cf. R. LATOURELLE, "Dei Verbum II: Commentary," 218.

[39] Ibid.

in this reciprocal exchange of love includes not only the faculties of the intellect and the will, but the particularity of the whole person, including their unique circumstances and manner of expressing themselves that accentuate their existential mode of returning to the Father during their pilgrimage of life in Christ. This dynamic is frequently emphasized in both preaching and in pastoral ministry, wherein the Father meets the person in the Word so that the person in their own particular manner, or mode, or pathway, may find his or herself inserted into the person of Christ, thus coming to discover, or grow more deeply, in the felt and lived experience of God's personal love for them. This pastoral and spiritual reality demands not only a theological but a metaphysical foundation.

One may certainly come to believe in God according to the natural path of seeing the stars in the night sky, which lifts his or her reason to the possibility of God's creative power (*Dei Filius*), and then with the assistance of the Holy Spirit to the act of faith. This natural methodology that involves preambles to the faith is most certainly valid, and remains a pathway to God. However, we believe, along with Joseph Ratzinger and the Fathers of the Second Vatican Council, that a more personal methodology is in required which reverses the order and places the primacy more on the person of the Father Himself recaching out to the person of the believer through the Holy Spirit. The Father does this so that the believer may come to know firstly perhaps through the experience of the act of faith in another person and the personal love of the Father who reaches out to his or her heart to stir one towards his love as this often first occurs through the love of that mediating person.

An experienced and felt awareness of the stirring (*Dei Verbum*) and the opening of the eyes often happens pastorally, not through seeing the stars in a night sky, but by encountering God in another person. Most frequently, according to our human, spiritual and pastoral experience, it is by the way of God stirring our hearts through a direct mediation, whether by the Person of Jesus Christ Himself in the form of a religious or spiritual encounter, wherein the Holy Spirit speaks to one's heart, or by the words or the faith experience of another trusted person which move one's heart to faith.

It is most often in a fellowship or community of believers where the first movements of faith occur in an adult. Certainly God sometimes reaches us in grace first through the primary use of our intellect, through the means of the less personal elements of nature. But for others, he speaks directly into the experience in a manner wherein reason is clearly not at the forefront, but a felt experience of direct communication or contact, which then leads the intellect to become more engaged with what was experienced. For some, the more natural manner of coming to know God in grace is sufficient. For many today, however, whether at the beginning or more mature phase of the spiritual life, something much more personal is needed. This seems especially true in the hearts of those desiring to cultivate an authentic life-long relationship with God in sustained, consistent, and surrendered prayer rooted in love, which is capable of authentically accepting at the same time the reality of his or her broken and sinful inner self. It also includes self-awareness and self-possession of accepting the particularity of one's own unique pathway, albeit within the obedience which Revelation demands. Furthermore, as this experience of the personal encounter with God is deepened, the contemplative pathway to communion with the Divine is marked by authentic acknowledging, relating and receiving from God in prayer.[40]

## 2.4 The Necessity for a Renewed Metaphysics

From what has been said regarding this emphasis on personhood, that is, both divine and human, a door is opened for a metaphysics to emerge which reflects, from the ontological perspective, the primacy of personhood, communion and love. The point of departure for such a metaphysics would be the invitation of the person of the Father to all of creation to partake in the event of communion.[41]

As we will see in Part Three Chapter Five, According to Maximus the Confessor, if the Father makes all things by his will, and he makes each creature by an act of his will, then the Father knows existing things as he knows the products of his own will. The will, in the classic Christian sense, is identified with the love of the Father, which is significantly distinct from the Father knowing things simply by their own nature (classic Greek philosophy). Maximus, makes the important and necessary theological observation that

---

[40] S. TRAYNOR, *The Parish as a School of Prayer*, Institute for Priestly Formation, Omaha, NE, 2013.

[41] Cf. INTERNATIONAL THEOLOGICAL COMMISSION, *Theology, Christology, Anthropology*, 1982-1983. "In ancient philosophy substance in general was at the center of things, but here the center is a 'metaphysic of charity,' namely, the person, whose most perfect act of charity is the act of charity."

God knows things only because he first loves them.[42] This opens the door for a metaphysic of love preceding knowledge. Maximus thus provides the foundations for a Christian metaphysic where love is the ultimate link between God and creation.

The Incarnation is an act of love by the Father, and this mandates that personhood and love must be understood as primary in any Christian metaphysic. Because love is the principle act of God in creation, love must be the human person's principal act of response. For love to be the primary response, faith must have access to the deepest existential corners of one's heart, involving one's *whole self.* These hidden places of the heart often remain shrouded in mystery, acknowledged, related, and healed only through the life of grace and prayer, void of concepts. Here, in an *apophatic* form of prayer that may be described as nothing less than loving surrender, one begins to see the mystery of the person emerge as a protagonist in the reception of Revelation, so as to grow spiritually and morally in his or her personal appropriation of the mystery according to the particularities of one's own personhood, always in obedience to the Father in the Son. Thus, it is evident that a renewed metaphysics be urgently sought in order to philosophically sustain these theological truths.

---

[42] Cf. MAXIMUS THE CONFESSOR, *Ambigua 7, On the Cosmic Mystery of Jesus Christ: Selected Writings from Saint Maximus the Confessor,* P.M. BLOWERS and R.L WILKEN, eds; 2003.

## 2.5 Pope Benedict and Pope Francis: Toward Personalism

While Part Four, Chapter Ten of this project will look deeper into selected elements of both the Pontificates of Pope Benedict and Pope Francis regarding the human person, it will be beneficial to introduce here the reality that the development that we have been tracing above is evidently seen in the more personalist approach to Revelation found in both Pontificates, which gives the reader a taste for a renewed metaphysic needed to justify such a development.

In his first encyclical, *Deus Caritas Est* (2005), Pope Benedict XVI was able to elaborate on his earlier theological contributions to *Dei Verbum* by restating the necessity of moving from a classical to a more personal understanding of God as he teaches:

> The divine power that Aristotle at the height of Greek philosophy sought to grasp through reflection, is indeed for every being an object and desire and love, and as an object of love this divinity moves the world, but in itself it lacks nothing and does not love: it is solely the object of love. The one God in whom Israel believes, on the other hand, loves with a personal love.[43]

In his second encyclical, *Spe Salvi* (2007), Pope Benedict XVI states that God's desire to reveal himself to the human person is not

---

[43] BENEDICT XVI, *Deus Caritas Est*, Encyclical, # 9, 2006.

simply a communication of things to be known, but it involves the whole person as he states:

> So now we can say: Christianity was not only 'good news' – the communication of a hitherto unknown content. In our language we would say: The Christian message was not only 'informative' but 'performative'. This means: The Gospel is not merely a communication of things that can be known – it is one that makes things happen and is life-changing.[44]

Pope Francis, in continuity with his predecessor uses the same hermeneutic when he speaks of the relationship of the *kerygma* to the transmission of the faith. He speaks of the initial encounter with God in Revelation giving the one who receives security, meaning, and wisdom, as it satisfies the thirst for the infinite. For this grace to occur, the Pope states, preaching should be more evangelical than philosophical. Essentially, the transmission of the faith should first be aimed at quenching a heart that thirsts, which fills the deepest corners of the human heart first with the person of God Himself, and thereafter, with more prayer, the necessary doctrine that expresses Him, and teaches us more about who He is in Himself. Pope Francis writes:

> We must not think that in catechesis the kerygma gives way to a supposedly more "solid" formation. Nothing is more solid, profound, secure, meaningful and wisdom-filled than

[44] BENEDICT XVI, *Spe Salvi*, Encyclical, # 3, 2007.

> that initial proclamation. All Christian formation consists of entering more deeply into the kerygma, which is reflected in and constantly illumines, the work of catechesis, thereby enabling us to understand more fully the significance of every subject which the latter treats. It is the message capable of responding to the desire for the infinite which abides in every human heart. The centrality of the kerygma calls for stressing those elements which are most needed today: it has to express God's saving love which precedes any moral and religious obligation on our part; it should not impose the truth but appeal to freedom; it should be marked by joy, encouragement, liveliness and a harmonious balance which will not reduce preaching to a few doctrines which are at times more philosophical than evangelical. All this demands on the part of the evangelizer certain attitudes which foster openness to the message: approachability, readiness for dialogue, patience, a warmth and welcome which is non-judgmental.[45]

Pastoral experience has shown us that at the beginning of the spiritual life one encounters God through the sacramental presence of the other, and at the same time as one grows in the spiritual life, one relates to God in a manner that moves more from concepts to personal presence. In prayer, one sits and is drawn into deeper and more prolonged moments of silence. At the same time the silence grows and deepens, so does the desire to share God with others. Yet,

[45] FRANCIS, *Evangelii Gaudium*, Apostolic Exhortation, # 165, 2013.

in this sharing of God with others, the otherness of God, in his great mystery, and at the same time his very imminent and personal love are so overwhelming, that concepts seem to not explain him well enough, and in themselves, one is aware that they do not quench the deeper thirst. It is at this period of the spiritual life that one must not abandon the intellectual, but to see and receive it in a more personal manner, so that it becomes ever more integrated with one's prayer and yet at the same time does not lose its doctrinal import.

This hermeneutic introduced by the Second Vatican Council as discussed in this chapter enables one to do just that. A methodology in theology that is rooted in the Divine Person of the Father speaking to the human person, is thus both for the beginner, the person seeking to be filled by God, and finding him in the sacramental encounter with other persons, as well as for the wise and experienced contemplative. The Fathers of the Second Vatican Council in discerning to describe how God relates with us in the totality of our personhood, with our minds and our hearts, only serves to plunge us more deeply into the mystery which is the Trinitarian God Himself, in whatever stage we may be in the spiritual journey. Furthermore, this theological methodology must rely upon a metaphysical foundation, or else it will not have lasting and practical import to the relationship between philosophy and theology.

It is for this reason that Part Two Chapter Four (Professor John Betz) and Part Three Chapter Five (Maximus the Confessor) are so imperative for a theological method and metaphysic to ground this contribution. In Part Two Chapter Four, Betz metaphysically vindicates the theological contribution of Ratzinger and the Second Vatican Council with his important project. Furthermore, in Part Three

Chapter Five, which is the metaphysical summit of our project, Eastern Patristic Father Saint Maximus the Confessor (580-622) will serve to provide a more detailed metaphysic to the now opened door in the methodology to be proposed in Part Two Chapter Four by Betz.

Before we look to Betz and Maximus, however, we now turn to the ongoing philosophical project of Professor David Walsh in Part Two Chapter Three in order to find an academic rooted in an ongoing search for personhood rooted in these theological principles. In Walsh's political and philosophical search, a deeper philosophical illumination of this theological reality is provided, as Walsh provides an even deeper existential glimpse into the mystery of personhood.

# PART TWO

## *OPENINGS*

## *PHILOSOPHICAL AND THEOLOGICAL OPENING*

# Chapter Three

# Professor David Walsh: The Person as the Summit of Modern Philosophy

"God created mankind in his image; in the image of God
he created them; male and female he created them."

(Gen 1:27)

## 3.1 The Reappropriation of Modern Philosophy

Walsh's *The Growth of the Liberal Soul* (1997), reaches its own summit when we realize that at the heart of the liberal construct is the recognition of persons as the center of value.[1] This leads Walsh to an even deeper historical and analytical review of modern philosophy as a whole in *The Modern Philosophical Revolution: The Luminosity of Existence*, (2008).[2] In this philosophical tome Walsh travels from the German Immanuel Kant (1724-1804) to the Danish Soren Kierkegaard (1813-1855) in a reappropriation of modern

[1] See D.WALSH, *The Priority of the Person*, University of Notre Dame Press, 2020. 48-49, and D. WALSH, *The Growth of the Liberal Soul*, University of Missouri Press, 1997.

[2] See D. WALSH, *The Modern Philosophical Revolution*, Cambridge University Press, 2008.

philosophy in its entirety as a search for existence and personhood. Each philosopher Walsh examines contributes to the search for personhood, some more fully than others, but each one contributes, and each one builds upon the other, despite the limitations of each. One can see as one follows Walsh on this journey that something illumining is happening in the mighty, somewhat flawed, and grace filled attempts of each of these thinkers to arrive towards illumined personhood.

Walsh's reappropriation of modern philosophy is a journey like we had never seen, and for which we had been longing, as the person begins to emerge, which we will propose, as sacramental. For too long we had seen modern philosophy as summarily dismissed by Catholic theology as being overly subjective without proper moorings, but this theological rejection of modern philosophy did not resonate with our theological discoveries in Part One, Chapter One, where the *state of the questions* clearly demands a deeper engagement with this period of philosophy. From a Classical and Christian perspective, one finds in these pages of Walsh a new dawn for the horizon of the human person, who is now called to live out of these Christian values so that order may resonate in society from the very source of personhood. Despite the limitations of Modern Philosophy, such as the rejection of the Fall and of Original Sin, Walsh nevertheless leads us to the conclusion that philosophical discussion should not be "about the person," but on the other hand, should emerge "out of the life of the person who speaks."[3]

[3] Ibid., 60.

### 3.1.1 KANT: THE PRIMACY OF THE PRACTICAL OVER THE THEORETICAL

Kant favored practical reason over theoretical reason, which resonates deeply with this project as we will look In Chapters Six through Eight to the contemporary Greek Orthodox theologian Metropolitan John Zizioulas to find the way in which truth is discovered in the lived experience of the Eucharist. This existential turn fundamentally locates ethics and life as primary. Our project provides the appropriate place for the lived reality of practical reason in the Holy Eucharist, because it is the place where knowledge and life fully intermingle with ontology.

Kant saves us from an abstract and theoretical kind of knowledge that does not fully include the person, and from the kind of knowledge that reduces the person to more of a subject without ontology, thus diminishing the objective value of the full illumination of personhood in the lived response. Walsh argues that Kant's intention to erect a critical foundation for metaphysics is actually metaphysical from the start, as Kant insists on the rights of reason to take further steps once its limits have been acknowledged.[4] Kant, according to Walsh, is animated by faith, as he was on a quest for a knowledge that transcended the boundaries of experience. While Kant was resolved to confine speculative reason solely within the limits of experience, Walsh argues, from a paradoxical perspective, that this philosophical position of Kant is due precisely to the depth

---

[4] D. WALSH, *The Modern Philosophical Revolution: Luminosity of Existence*, Cambridge University Press, 2008, 31.

of his faith in what cannot be known experientially.[5] Walsh argues that Kant does not so much as deny the mysteries of dogma as he radically eliminates all objective reference to dogma, but on the other hand merely argues that we cannot know the mysteries beyond our own participation in them. The background for this argument for religion within the limits of reason is the Enlightenment critique of the superstitious use of religion,[6] which Kant would have respected and therefore desired to use reason to defend religion in a purely rational manner.

Rights language is in the realm of reason, and Kant opens up a philosophical revolution when he recognizes that the language of rights refers not to the natural world, but to the luminous and mysterious reality within which we exist. As rights are transcendent for Kant, the transcendent dimension of personhood is clearly captured in this understanding. He opens up the existential perspective in philosophy.[7] We are so familiar with the language of rights today, and use the language so frequently, that the excessive familiarity actually becomes an obstacle to realizing its existential status.[8] From an epistemological perspective, we are invited to follow Kant in his strain against theoretical dominance within the language of rights so that we may be able to recognize the authoritative truth within which theory itself has its place.[9] We thus find ourselves within the mystery of the person, transcendent and possessing rights, wherein

[5] Ibid., 31.

[6] Ibid., 57.

[7] Ibid., 76.

[8] Ibid., 67.

[9] Ibid., 71.

the person is invited to respond in truth within the context of society and to Revelation itself with a disposition of trust and faith.

### 3.1.2 Hegel: The Inwardness of the Human Person within History

Georg Wilhelm Friederich Hegel (1770-1831) advocated for the priority of the process over the end, thus emphasizing inwardness, or more specifically the inwardness of the person, within history, as he followed the existential lead from Kant.[10] The meaning of the parts can only be understood in the context of the expansion of movement that started at the beginning. Hegel comes to arrive in his later years at understanding philosophy itself as an infinite movement in which religion finds its fulfillment. Philosophy acquires an existential character for Hegel in his realization that philosophy must be oriented toward life, faith and love. The inner spiritual ferment of modernity was leading him beyond the medieval past, the feudalism in France, or the imperialism in Germany, and into the future, marked by his account of the French Revolution as being a "glorious mental dawn."[11] Hegel desires a non-conformist approach to religion, and desires an authentic faith, lived within the light of divinity, as he saw that the Pietism movement had significant limitations and reached its success only by achieving recognition within the State.[12] The crisis of Pietism made visible for Hegel a deeper

---

[10]Ibid., 76-77.

[11] Ibid., 81. Here Walsh cites Hegel's Philosophy of History.

[12]Ibid., 82-83. Pietism was a reform movement within Protestant Churches in the late 17th Century in Germany and Switzerland that sought

crisis of Christianity, which is that the external observance of divine commands were not alone sufficient.[13] The spirit for Hegel is revealed in the person as a form of divine self-realization, and in Christ he finds an immediate existence revealing to the human person the spiritual or existential mode of knowing God.[14] In Hegel's project the object of knowledge evaporates in the reality of the human person living a life in God.[15] Hegel thus had a drive to remain strictly faithful to the inner dynamic of the spirit,[16] seeing the spirit as an opportunity for growth and spiritual development.

### 3.1.3 Schelling: and Nietzsche: Philosophy as Beyond Books and Person as Prior to Morality

As Friederich Wilhem Joseph von Schelling (1775-1874) argued that philosophy could no longer be contained in books, but by the whole of one's self entered into it,[17] he may be reduced historically, along with Friedrich Nietzsche (1844-1900), as merely another participant within the logic of the philosophical turn toward existence that began with Kant.[18] Nietzsche, for example, categorized as a nihilist, on the contrary sought a manner, according to Walsh, with

---

to promote personal piety, spiritual renewal, and practical Christianity, emphasizing individual faith experiences and a direct relationship with God.

[13] Ibid., 83.

[14] Ibid., 107-108.

[15] Ibid., 109.

[16] Ibid., 129.

[17] Ibid., 176-178.

[18] Ibid., 179.

which to actually overcome nihilism.[19] While intending to discard virtually all terminology on morality and metaphysics, Nietzsche does so only to render existence more transparent. Nietzsche and Schelling inchoately knew that it is essential for existence to first emerge before morality and metaphysics, as the person must be primary.

With these thinkers, truth must not be understood as a correspondence between a subject and an object, but the mode of existence within which one lives. As for Schelling, luminosity was only able to be understood because one as a person lives within that reality. The insuperable boundaries of an order needed to be overcome, to exalt the person through whom all truth is known. Schelling did his best to describe this in a language of metaphysics without metaphysics. Philosophy cannot be understood from the outside, but only from within, as a participant within its very unfolding.[20]

### 3.1.4 Heidegger: Philosophy Outside of the Academy

Martin Heidegger (1889-1976) observed that at the turn of the century, philosophy had been reaching a low point after Nietzsche and was returning to the halls of the German University, thus tragically becoming divorced from life again. Heidegger, despite being in University life, maintained, not unlike Nietzsche, that philosophy could only be done outside of the University. From his early years he looked outside of the philosophical Academy towards a horizon

---

[19] Ibid., 179.

[20] Ibid., 178-181.

of greater vitality, and to those whose work ruptured the sterile placidity.[21] With his landmark work *Being and Time* of 1947, he engaged in a quest for being. The period called for a philosophical retrieval of a primordial inquiry into being itself. Heidegger was convinced in his search that a discovery of being would open up access to the human person, but Walsh astutely notes that it was here that he missed the point, it should have been the other way around, as it is only the person who is able to open our understanding of being.[22] Heidegger had the noble desire of rescuing the subject from its isolation in a world of objects and was successful in many regards of this rescue of the subject, but he never returns to the primordiality of the social whole.[23] This, according to Walsh, disconnected his project from ethics and life.

### 3.1.5 Levinas: Ethics Prior to Ontology

While the French Emmanuel Levinas (1906-1995) does not directly influence Zizioulas, here we have another example of reciprocal convergence, as one will find in Part Three (Chapters Six, Seven and Eight) that Zizioulas will provide a theological home for Levinas's philosophical intuitions (albeit from an ontological perspective). The French Jewish Levinas breaks from his mentor Heidegger, and declares for the first time that ethics is prior to ontology.[24] This is a noticeable philosophical discovery for our project,

[21] Ibid., 235.

[22] Ibid., 246.

[23] Ibid., 248.

[24] Ibid., 292

and one that Zizioulas will implicitly appreciate philosophically, but wholly address theologically, that is, the understanding that otherness is discovered in the ethic of life, and must be a point of departure for epistemology. To truly be itself, Levinas argues, the "I" exists insofar as it is in transcendence toward the other. Alone, the "I" remains enchained in its own *hypostasis*.[25] Here, Levinas and Zizioulas are similar insofar as their approach to otherness is essential to being.

There are, however, divergences between Levinas and Zizioulas, as Levinas's thought leads more toward the ethical and self-giving, and Zizioulas's thought toward the ontologically personal. Zizioulas is providentially capable of theologically completing the philosophical openings in Levinas, as we will propose in Part Three Chapters Six through Eight with Zizioulas. Zizioulas proposes a liturgical communion as an ontological and eschatological finality so as to properly answer the question of otherness in creation. From a purely philosophical perspective, with this understanding of the other, Levinas, according to Walsh, effects a breakthrough as Walsh writes:

> It is because Levinas starts with otherness, specifically with the preeminent otherness of the other, that the absurd no longer exists. Transcendence has hitherto been the goal of philosophy, but it has remained a transcendence within the grasp of the self. Levinas, by contrast, begins with the other, the superabundance of meaning that is already there before the movement toward exteriority even begins. Only the

---

[25] Ibid., 298.

> relationship with a person, an other, can properly constitute a transcendence by means of a distance that is surpassed and restrained at the same time.[26]

Discourse, or the dialogical, whether between persons, or between the person and God, involves the overcoming of separation and at the same time preserves otherness. If we are to communicate, we must have otherness. For Levinas, a philosophy of revelation implies a philosophy of discourse. It is precisely in this opening toward the other, that the infinity of freedom is disclosed,[27] and responsibility constitutes its reality as freedom when it aims not to possess, but to reach what is beyond reaching.[28] Levinas's contribution is a "metaphysic of otherness."[29]

### 3.1.6 Derrida: The Personal as Beyond Identification

The French-Algerian Jacques Derrida (1930-2004) subsequently begins to deconstruct this culminating point of German Idealism as found in Levinas. Just when a coherent structure may be forming, Derrida takes the project back to the beginning as he definitively rejects any theoretical coherence that may have been accrued along the way with the thinkers who preceded him.[30] He identifies the total failure of language because language contains the unsurpassable

---

[26] Ibid., 301-302.
[27] Ibid., 302-303.
[28] Ibid., 310.
[29] Ibid., 313.
[30] Ibid., 335.

boundary that cannot include itself, because the personal escapes all attempts at identification. The failure of language thus becomes the possibility of language. Even using the word 'God' escapes our capacity to define him. This opens up the *apophatic* dimension of language, and makes language universal, insofar as it always exceeds what it contains, and thus has the potential to be translated universally. Meaning is universalized because a singular word is never capable of fully conveying want it wants to convey. A community is always needed that is greater than its native tongue, so that it pushes the understanding of the word towards a more communal understanding,[31] again always involving the other, and in this case pushing language beyond itself and pointing to the need for a community beyond itself. In the *difference*, every attempt at singularity escapes its identification.[32] One community alone cannot contain the fullness of truth, but diverse geographic and linguistic communities are needed, which in our opinion informs the philosophical foundation for the theological principle of "catholic:" and of "unity in diversity." For example, the Armenian Church in Turkey needs the Coptic Church in Egypt , along with the Roman Church in the West with the Pope, to live in its fullness.

### 3.1.7 Kierkegaard: The Arrival at Life over Discourse

Walsh places the Danish Soren Kierkegaard (1813-1855) out of chronological order in his treatment of modern philosophers so as

[31] Ibid., 381.

[32] Ibid., 419.

to highlight the genius of his contribution, and to suggest that he was potentially overlooked.[33] Connected with the Continental French and German philosophers, yet distinct from them, he wrote short articles in a language (Dutch) not followed by the Continental philosophers.[34] Heidegger, after his *Being and Time*, labeled Kierkegaard a "religious thinker" so as to dismiss him.[35] Heidegger, Levinas, and Derrida all took good note of him, but did not find him as a contributor furthering the conversation.[36] With this Kierkegaard, now was the time to live, and not just talk about living.[37]

Kierkegaard, following Socrates, preferred living over writing. Like Socrates, he understood the call to live out the struggle which the philosopher addresses.[38] He did not merely desire to proclaim truth, but to live it in existence. He regarded himself as the reader of his books, not the author. He only wrote secondarily for other people, and primarily for himself, and had a much greater self-opening than Nietzsche, as he understood the need for the other.[39] He was not preoccupied and limited by the self, but knew that the existential points back to the single person. For this great philosopher in his *Fear and Trembling*, a human being is not just part of the whole; he is also a *part that contains the whole*.[40] Kierkegaard arrives at this

---

[33] Ibid., 391.

[34] Ibid.

[35] Ibid., 392-393.

[36] Ibid., 393-394.

[37] Ibid., 395.

[38] Ibid., 396-397.

[39] Ibid., 399.

[40] Ibid., 419.

groundbreaking and revolutionary understanding of personhood, that *the part contains the whole*, and that the *whole is in the part*. David Walsh maintains the same, and states that as the person is clearly transcendent, and understands, with us, that the only manner for which transcendence may be present in time is in Jesus Christ.

Kierkegaard becomes a significant influence and catalyst for Walsh in his *Politics of the Person as the Politics of Being* (2016) wherein Walsh pierces the perennial problem for metaphysical philosophy which begins at the First Council of Nicaea (325) which made a doctrinal affirmation with the use of the language of substance (*homoousious*). While this was a necessary and foundational definition for dogmatic theology, to declare that the eternal Son of God shares in the same substance with the Father, it did not help to advance the language of persons in relation to other persons (*hypostasis*), as the relational term *hypostasis* would have stressed more the relation between persons, and would have given more philosophical precision to personhood.[41] To make matters more complicated, the great Italian Scholastic Doctor of the Church, Saint Thomas Aquinas (1225-1274), understands that the person is something more than nature, but Aquinas was restricted in remaining within the language of substance to explain his understanding of personhood.[42] In his *Prima Pars* of the *Summa Theologica*, Question 30, article 4, Saint Thomas states that the person is not given to signify the

---

[41] D. WALSH, *Politics of the Person as the Politics of Being*, University of Notre Dame Press, 2016, 17-18.

[42] Ibid., 12.

individual as part of the nature, but the subsistent reality in that nature.[43] When Saint Thomas understands person as "subsistent reality" he is clearly pointing to something beyond, something transcendent. Saint Thomas uses the language of substance in an attempt to define personhood but he remains unable to define it in a way other than by substance, which, in effect, limits our understanding of personhood. For the person exists only in a mode of reality which is not totally circumscribed by nature, which is why our project needs the theologian Zizioulas (Part Three Chapter Six through Eight) for an understanding of the person in an eschatological context, that is, within a mode of being which is beyond the natural, but rather personal and eschatological.

## 3.2 God As Beyond the Genus of Being

From a Western perspective, Bishop Robert Barron explains that God is identified as "Being itself."[44] Barron posits that Saint Thomas makes a decisive point when he says that God is not *ens summum* (highest being), but *ipsum esse subsistens*, which is the sheer act of Being itself.[45] More specifically, Barron states that for Saint Thomas, God cannot be defined or situated within any *genus*.[46] Saint

---

[43] T. AQUINAS, *Summa Theologica*, I,I, 30, 4.

[44] R. BARRON, *Exploring Catholic Theology*, Baker Academic, 2015, 66.

[45] R. BARRON, *Seeds of the Word*, Word on Fire Publications, 2015, 233-234. "The Maker of the entire Universe cannot be something within the Universe."

[46] R. BARRON, *Catholicism*, Word on Fire Publications, 2025, 63.

Maximus the Confessor goes even further than Saint Thomas, however, and maintains that God stands above being. For Barron the "I am Who Am" of Exodus 3:14 maintains that God is the sheer act of existence, the act of being itself.[47]

Barron captures something important from a Western perspective that has not been captured nearly enough due to Western metaphysical limitations, that of God continuously creating, as opposed to a once and for all act. An ever present and ever new act is always being poured out of the divine source. Barron attributes this to Saint Thomas insofar as Saint Thomas describes creation as *quaedam relatio ad Creatorem cum novitiate essendi* (a relationship to the Creator with freshness of being). To capture this reality more dynamically, however, we argue that Saint Maximus the Confessor is needed (Part Three Chapter Five), with his distinction between the *Logos* and the *logoi*, to see more clearly this reality that Saint Thomas desired to make known; that is, that the Creator is continually drawing the person from non-being to being, thus making the person new.[48] Barron notes that the true God can enter into the most intimate ontological unity with a creature, and the result is not a diminution of the person, but rather an enhancement of creaturely being. Barron continues by stating that God and the creature are capable of an ontological coherence, and being-in-the-other, so that each can let the other be other even as they enter into the closest contact.[49]

---

[47] R. BARRON, *An Now I See*, Word on Fire Academic Publications, 2021, 133-134.

[48] Ibid., 141.

[49] R. BARRON, *The Priority of Christ*, Baker Academic, 2021, 56.

Our project seeks to bring the person into this horizon that Saint Thomas identifies with God. Our aim is to bring the human person now into this dynamic of an ever present God who continually pours life into being, not usurping nature, but rather dynamically sustaining it, and by way of either *metaxy* or analogy to better explain this participation. To claim with Professor Walsh that "being is one person" we will however need more philosophical and theological assistance from the East, as the West is not capable on its own of taking this next step into the sacramentality of personhood.

## 3.3 The Unsurpassable Horizon of Persons

A shift from the language of subjects and objects to the unsurpassable horizon of persons will help philosophy overcome this linguistic deficiency. Persons always transcend place and time, they are always beyond being, but at the same time they do not exist outside of the circumstances of daily life. Scientific method becomes defective insofar as it overlooks the actual person of the scientist who is presenting the hypothesis. Everything begins and returns to the person.[50] Our Christian experience demands the acceptance that the other is closer to me than I am to myself. Therefore, the only manner in which to understand freedom properly and fully is found in the opening to the other.[51] Walsh captures well that we cannot escape this profound metaphysical reality. Persons alone are capable of standing within and providing access to the whole, albeit without

---

[50] D.WALSH, *Politics of the Person as the Politics of Being*, 98-101.

[51] Ibid., 13.

naming it, since they themselves are contained by it.[52] Walsh describes the reality within which Saint Thomas was standing as his own reflection on personhood, but unable to name it linguistically, because he himself was contained by the mystery, which rendered it undefinable. Plato as well, Walsh observes, failed to anchor the beautiful in the horizon of the person. The person is the center of the universe, in each we behold the whole world because each is beyond the whole world.[53]

Walsh uncovers the fact that substance and self-subsistence become a philosophical thicket because personhood is not placed first. An ambiguous idea of substance, Walsh boldly and accurately notes, was transmitted by the Classical and Medieval traditions.[54] In turn, Walsh's project demands that philosophy must become capable of articulating the horizon of the person. The existential reality illustrated by Walsh is that the other is closer to me than I am to myself, and therefore Walsh stands at the summit of all of Modern Philosophy when he defines that the only way to understand freedom properly and fully is in the context of an opening toward the other.[55] When the other depends entirely on me, their call necessarily penetrates the whole of me.[56] The political theory of David Walsh becomes imperative because, community is a metaphysical necessity,[57] and Walsh understands personhood and community to be

[52] Ibid., 102.

[53] Ibid., 145-147.

[54] Ibid., 27-29.

[55] Ibid., 30-31.

[56] Ibid., 45.

[57] Ibid., 51

inseparable. Walsh observes that in the post Modern and post Christian denial of metaphysics, we are attempting to rescue the autonomous person, but in the end this places us on the verge of the disappearance of the person. When Walsh discovers that persons are actually the point at which nature arrives at its culmination, we arrive at an illuminating brilliance, as Walsh is the first philosopher capable of describing that when a person stands within the whole, it is radically different from how other created beings stand within the whole, because only persons can know that they stand within the whole.

The persons themselves, he states, cannot give a definition to being, but they have more knowledge than other irrational participants. Even if the human person renounces metaphysics, they have to take it seriously enough intellectually to renounce it.[58] Walsh concludes that Being can only be put it into question by persons because the person alone is not what he or she is, as again, persons themselves think within the horizon of thought and thinking is only possible by persons. Capturing that thinking occurs within the rationality of the person, opened to the transcendent, Walsh posits that the thinking person is not included in that what is thought about because the thinking person transcends it.[59] We can hereby see why knowledge and the intellect is so important to the human person, because knowledge attests to the metaphysical horizon within which it is, which pushes us towards ethics for its actualization in the realm

[58] Ibid., 102-103.

[59] Ibid., 27.

of responsibility, without every diminishing ontology.[60] Walsh achieves, therefore, a great reconciliation between the subjective and the objective in his project that no other Modern Philosopher was able to achieve, which deemed the whole project of Modern Philosophy a failure in objectivity, but in Walsh's reappropriation he provides us with not only a new method with which to read the Moderns, but an illumined and brilliant conclusion which captures each of their deepest desires in a manner which they would have never imagined.

## 3.4 Art as a Manifestation of Personhood

Walsh argues that art is the best example of this reality of personhood, as it proceeds from the horizon of the idea that takes hold of the artist, as if from a horizon.[61] Art is what transcends analysis, and only a human person is capable of reading into the subtle nuances of art, or the subtle nuances of inter-personal relationship and dialogue that disclose the deeper reality of something the other is trying to convey in words, but at the same time the words are alluding them. Walsh notes that art is the mutual permeability of the material and the spiritual, which is essential for grasping the metaphysical truth of personhood, as existence in a material universe is deepened through the integration that art brings. Walsh values art so highly because it helps us realize that we live in a world not of fixed

---

[60] Ibid., 78-86.

[61] Ibid., 157.

quantifiable objects, but of the fluidity for the disclosure of mysteries to the human person found within it, which is central to his project.

With this understanding, Walsh is able to observe that poetry, for example, can therefore often say more than physics about the universe in which we find ourselves, as poetry, as an art, is able to access the inaccessible because it operates within the personal horizon. A non-present presence hovers continually in art, as Zizioulas also theologically will claim the same mysterious reality of art theologically as presence in absence understood through personhood (Part Four Chapters Six through Eight). Art, for Walsh, addresses each person in his or her utterly irreplaceable inwardness. Persons, for Walsh, are the interpreters of art as the disclosures of being, and for Zizioulas the *icon* (Part Three, Chapter Eight), which bears the eschatological presence of personhood, fully theologically completes this philosophical insight of Walsh.

This thirst to connect truth with the personal is what led us to our third project, *Theology as Prayer* (2022), because we wanted to illustrate how ten theologians of the Catholic Church could take root in the spiritual life of an individual person, in a manner where the truth of the theology was assimilated into the truth of the person, through the lens of beauty, according to one's own particularity.[62] Art makes matter come alive in the museums and the world, and similarly the believer makes theology come alive by appropriating it and allowing it to be integrated into the particularity of his or her personhood. Music is like art insofar as the person is made present

---

[62] J. CUSH and W.R. OXLEY, *Theology as Prayer*, Institute for Priestly Formation, 2022.

in the physical space that we inhabit, and yet that person who created the music is not contained by it and does not belong within it. Both Walsh (philosophically) and Zizioulas (theologically) capture that art is the gift of self-giving, made permanent in material. Theologically, we will find in Zizioulas (Part Four, Chapter Eight), that the Eucharist, similarly, provides us with an enduring ontology in the material, in the celebration wherein matter is transformed. In Part Four, Chapter Eight, we will discover that in the Eucharist, like persons receiving art, we find the oscillation between the closure and disclosure of personhood, as beauty is glimpsed, received and understood. For Walsh, art is always greater, it points to metaphor, and only the human person is capable of the intuitive intelligence of comprehending metaphor.

## 3.5 The Person as Prior to Being

Walsh, in his *The Politics of the Person as the Politics of Being* (2016), aims to sketch a recentering of reality within the person. Instead of seeing the person within reality, Walsh now guides us in switching seats and finding the whole of reality within the person. Now, if a person is not reducible to the subjective, which indeed the person is not, than this position is not about embracing a radically subjectivist perspective. Ironically, Walsh notes, the person can be subjective only because the person is not defined by what he or she is; the person can transcend his or herself. Persons alone, Walsh captures, can behold their own subjectivity, of looking at themselves from outside of themselves, demonstrating that they are able to be objective about themselves. Walsh therefore concludes that every person is the unique pivot of the whole of reality,[63] and this is how we are obliged to responsibly relate to each person, with undivided attention, understanding, and compassionate listening, because each person carries the whole in themselves. It is our observation that pastorally, as we apply philosophy to lived theology, we always stand before the mystery and sacredness of personhood, yet without a justifying metaphysical foundation. We indeed know intuitively, and choose to live, like the person exceeds all metaphysical categories, but we do not have the language to describe this reality.[64]

Walsh, with Kierkegaard, and in a purely philosophical manner, understands God to be the seal of all that is personal. Walsh philosophically understands that only God gives the ontology. Furthermore, Walsh necessarily concludes that to stand within the question of God is to stand within what is "beyond being." Because personhood is the event of being, only a person can set his or her self aside, so that being might be. Only the person has the capacity to explain being. This philosophical conclusion provided by Walsh is truly groundbreaking, as it was something Saint Thomas and the Moderns could not achieve. The person is now the event of being. The person is the highest perspective for apprehending being. In fact, Walsh comprehends, as does Saint Maximus the Confessor (Part Three, Chapter Five), that each person embraces the whole of reality. Walsh can boldly conclude and declare that the truth of being is "one person."[65]

---

[63] D.WALSH, *Politics of the Person as the Politics of Being*, 18
[64] Ibid.
[65] Ibid., 98-101.

The person cannot be contained within being but rather is limitless transparence. The person is beyond being and is in his or her self as the encompassing ontology insofar as the person participates in the being of God who is the all-encompassing ontology. As the person stands outside being, we can thus claim that being and reality are only able to be found and discovered through personhood. Walsh therefore philosophically forces the rational and objective acceptance that persons exceed all other reality, which masterfully finally reconciles the subjective with the objective, which hitherto had been relegated to a philosophical thicket unable to be surpassed.

The person is a mystery and a deep abyss. As determined in Part One, the person must go out of oneself to discover oneself, and after going out, the person returns within and grows deeper in self-knowledge and self-awareness in turn.[66] All the while a person grows in self-awareness, and journeys deeper into their deepest center where God dwells, the person always remains a mystery unfathomable even to his or her self. Persons are thus uniquely singular in this regard. The person is limitless self-enactment and self-disclosure. A person is a whole within his or her self, and who the person is, is wholly contained within.

When Walsh states for the first time that Saint Thomas must first be a person to know how to speak about substance, it marked the first time we had heard of such an astounding truth articulated clearly. Up to the point of discovering Walsh's understanding of substance, we had been left helpless in its articulation. This lead us

---

[66] J.R. BETZ, *Christ the Logos of Creation: An Essay in Analogical Metaphysics, Renewal within the Tradition*, Emmaus Academic, 2023, 153.

to understand that Saint Thomas, as a PERSON, discerned that substance cannot fully define personhood, as he knew through his use of language that the person cannot be defined by nature, and that the human person escapes all identification and is uncapturable. It is the PERSON understanding the limitations and possibilities of substance that changes everything and brings hope.

Every person mysteriously exceeds the universal as the part is always greater than the whole, but every part needs the whole for its encompassing ontology. If a person looks to creation, the person can find his or her self, because, by way of analogy, there is something of the trajectory of personhood in all things. We can state with both Walsh (philosophically) and Saint Maximus the Confessor (theologically), that the lens of personhood gives meaning to all creation. At the same time, persons are the disclosure of which everything aims, and the highest point of that which is. Each person embraces the whole of reality, and the concept of being, as sought by the modern philosophers, is actually ONE person, but it is a search for an end upon which the moderns never arrived, as we argue that only theology is capable of fulfilling the quest.

## 3.6 Truth as Personal

There is nothing more real than personhood. Truth is inextricably personal. One cannot apprehend the truth in an impersonal manner. Personhood is unsurpassable mystery. Walsh finds in German idealism an open door for the inexorable search for personhood leading to what Walsh describes as the mystic's self-understanding within God becoming the project of a philosophy of the person articulated in the language of the person. German idealism draws from intuition. Unfortunately, however, as Walsh astutely clarifies, the German idealists understood the centrality of the person in the metaphysical dynamic, but as they did not have a personalist language, they fall back on the reified metaphysics that they desired to replace. Heidegger, for example, has a fully personalist philosophy without the acknowledgment of persons, and overlooks being as personal. Heidegger exclusively focuses on being, which Walsh says is a damning indictment of philosophical disorientation because persons are marginalized for an exclusive focus on being. Heidegger 's flaw, according to Walsh, is that he overlooks being as personal.[67]

The Father reveals himself personally to each one of us, which is the crux of Joseph Ratzinger's theology of Revelation, captured deeply in the Dogmatic Constitution on Divine Revelation, *Dei Verbum*, as described in Part One Chapter Two of this project. Each person is a unique recipient of God's Self-Revelation. We biblically conclude that the Revelation of God's name to Moses at the Burning Bush in Exodus Chapter Three as "I Am" is extended in grace to every recipient of Divine Revelation. Coupled with Walsh's philosophy of one person, and each and every person, containing the whole, being and exceeding the whole, the smallest and the frailest among us are an incalculable treasure because unfathomable rights are given to the smallest and weakest person out of love, which

[67] D.WALSH, *Politics of the Person as the Politics of Being*, 174-179.

manifests how precious and valuable each person is, beginning in the womb as created by God.[68]

## 3.7 The Person as Whole of Wholes

As Walsh understands that the person is the whole which contains all of the others, the person never competes for space with other beings because the person transcends the mode of presence that characterizes other beings.[69] Furthermore, we conclude with Walsh that the particularity of the person is something that is only granted by ontology. As introduced above in Part Three, Chapters Six through Eight, we will examine and apply the thought of Zizioulas through his description of the *ecclesial hypostasis* wherein this reality will be described from the perspective of grace (Chapter Seven), but first here with Walsh we have discovered the mystery applied philosophically.

Nature cannot contain the person, because the person continually overflows the boundaries in the direction of the whole as each person is the whole. All of existence, and the universe of particularities, is contained in each person. The particularities of each person are personally submersed in the whole that is God. This is what makes possible a world of persons, a WHOLE of WHOLES. Each person is the WHOLE universe in his or her self, and also an end in his or her self, and beyond the collective WHOLE. Each person, we

---

[68] Ibid., 44-52 and 254. Here Walsh frames the abortion argument in the language of the most unfathomable rights given to the smallest of persons out of love.

[69] Ibid., 246-256.

argue based in Walsh, is thus a WHOLE opened to other WHOLES.[70]

## 3.8 Love as Being

Love becomes an existential term for Walsh that may be equated with being because it is the only way each WHOLE may be open up to other WHOLES.[71] Relating in love is both objective and ontological. As Walsh observes that the person is "beyond being" because only the person can contemplate oneself,[72] at the same time the person only possesses his or her self by giving oneself to another in love. Love is the only link that truly existentially unites one subjective person with another subjective person, because love is ontological and defines God.

Too grasp this we first must understand God as a Family of Three defined by love. We will thus need Metropolitan Zizioulas to assist us in finding theologically that otherness is an ontological category within God, which will theologically fulfill this discovery of Walsh. The East helps us with understanding that God is first Three, a Trinity, before He is One (Part Three, Chapter Seven). God is first relational being, which Zizioulas draws from the theological font of the Cappadocian Fathers thus, establishing a theological methodology that is first Triune, differing from the methodology of Saint Thomas Aquinas and the West at large.

---

[70] Cf. D. WALSH, *The Priority of the Person: Political, Philosophical and Historical Discoveries*, University of Notre Dame, 2020, 15.

[71] Ibid., 251-253.

[72] Ibid., 19-22.

A deep process of self-discovery and awareness occurs when we give ourselves over to God, who is totally other, and to the other person in love. Persons are the apex of creation, and each person may truly be understood as the center of the universe but only in the context of the whole, which is defined existentially, ontologically and objectively by love. As all of existence, the universe of particularities, is contained in each person. We have come to observe that as the secular person tends towards expressing his or her self in particular methods of self-definition rooted in nature, for example, a bodily tattoo. Ontology, on the other hand, demands that particularities are understood only within the WHOLE that is God. This is what makes the above description of a whole of wholes possible.[73]

While the person might seek a bodily tattoo for identity, without first going out of themselves into God and the other person, their neighbor, the attempt is futile and tragically ends in death and thus is ontologically barren. That is, the tattoo dies with the body and thus the tattoo is incapable of providing true ontological otherness and identity. Each person therefore is indeed a whole opened to other wholes for true ontology to be given. Love alone is the link from one whole to another whole, and so we have come to conclude with the help of both Walsh and Saint Maximus the Confessor (Part Three, Chapter Five), that love may be classified as being, and have come to understand love as the ontological, existential, and epistemological link from one whole to another. Therefore, when the whole of one is submersed in the whole of the other, nothing of

---

[73] Ibid., 123-155.

particularity is lost, and the only manner that this may subjectively and objectively occur is according to the truth of love as being.

## 3.9 Evil as Non-Being

Conversely, evil may thus be understood as unreality, or non-being, because even before it is manifest God's love surpasses it.[74] God is in no way the cause of moral or physical evil. Evil is an absence or privation of God that is outside of the order of creation, it acts like a parasite on persons. God does not interfere with the free will of the human person, and physical and moral evils are brought about by sin alone, which may be understood as the cooperation in non-being. Evil is always a definitive turn away from reality. One must always turn toward the other to live in freedom and avoid the nothingness of evil, and to turn to the pain of the other is to turn toward truth and to place ourselves in the other. Walsh understands sympathy to be the bond of love that opens us to the deepest knowledge of the other.[75] With the existential category of sympathy elevated by Walsh to this objective level, we are able to more clearly see that love is not a possibility of being, but being itself, so that when we step out of the horizon of love, we step outside of being itself. For example, when a person is approached only objectively in the truth, thus lacking the existential sympathy which is love, the encounter is either lost or destroyed.

---

[74] Ibid., 53-86.
[75] Ibid., 202.

The most decisive aspects of personhood are only revealed within the three Divine Persons of God, as therefore we will need Zizioulas to capture the ontological otherness gleaned from the Cappadocian Fathers in their theology of the Trinity as essential for theological deepening these philosophical discoveries. In this regard, the baptized person, which Zizioulas describes as the *ecclesial hypostasis*, is granted the absolute fullness of this ontology.[76]

## 3.10 Eric Voegelin: The Person as the Lens of History

Now with Walsh we turn to history. Here we see the German American political philosopher Eric Voegelin's (1901-1985) influence on Walsh. Under Voegelin's direction, and for his doctoral dissertation, which became his first book, Walsh published *The Mysticism of Innerworldly Fulfillment: A Study of Jakob Bohme* (1983).[77] This, his first book, according to Professor David Sollenberger, Walsh late in his career evinces and undergoes more of an intellectual evolution from Voegelin into his own course of thought with his *After Ideology* (1990).[78] Sollenberger argues that Walsh was

---

[76] Ibid., 123-155.

[77] Professor Walsh did discover Jacob Boehme independently from Professor Voegelin. A critical section on Hegel was also originally included in this manuscript, though never published. As Walsh's thought become more developed over time, his philosophical regard for Hegel became more positive, unlike that of Voegelin.

[78] D. SOLLENBERGER, *The Experiential Roots of the Innerworldly: The Place of Jakob Bohme in David Walsh's Personalism*, in Personalism

insightful to see that the German Christian philosopher Jakob Boehme's (1575-1624) mystical philosophy was captured at this early stage in Walsh's career as being central to modernity and modern philosophy.[79] Voegelin's great philosophical achievement was in helping philosophy to remember that existence within history is the contribution of a Hebraic understanding of history. History, according to Voegelin, with this contribution, is now called to be read through the lens of an openness of persons to one other, insofar as truth is understood from this mindset as the connection of persons in the past, with the relational knowability occurring in the present. This of course is the gateway to the Christian understanding of history in the person of Jesus Christ. Only persons can exceed their moment in history and thus become capable of historical significance. The discovery of persons is bound up with both our fresh discovery and new understanding of history. Voegelin, and in turn Walsh, have both captured in their own particular ways the necessary predominance of personhood in history. Essentially, persons are needed for history to be history. Kierkegaard observed that historical research serves only as a propaedeutic to interior encounter. This is because the whole of history becomes transparent only through the inwardness of the person, and when this happens, the person becomes the pivot of history.

The inwardness of the historical person, therefore for Voegelin and Walsh, is indispensable to the discovery of history. Israel carried

---

for the 21st Century: Essays in Honor of David Walsh, Eds. T. HOLMAN and R. AVRAMENKO, Lexington Books, 2025, 53-57.

[79] Ibid., 57.

a transcendent message but still lacked the ontology to become a community wholly constituted by transcendence, because for this to occur the person in history must be identical with the transcendence as such, and only Jesus Christ is able to accomplish this. Voegelin and Walsh both have highlighted that the only way, therefore, that transcendence can be present in time is through Jesus Christ, and that with Jesus Christ, history emerges anew as the horizon of the person.[80] Transcendence speaking to transcendence through the lens of personhood, across history, is its truth. In the horrors of the ideology of the Nazi concentration camps, observes Victor Frankl, persons surmounted the suffering through a transcendent vision, which made them free, and their captors prisoners. The truth of personhood therefore prevailed in the darkest abyss of modern history.

Persons transcend place and time, and therefore are "beyond being,"[81] but they are always situated as existing within the circumstances of their setting in life.[82] Truth therefore arises through the dialogical process by which truth ever emerges but is at the same time not determined by it. We will discover with Zizioulas the importance of the Holy Eucharist as an ongoing encounter of dialogically mediated truth (Part Four, Chapter Eight), a daily conversation of the Father with the human person with and in Christ. Similarly, within the political community, we are furnished with the material for philosophical reflection because the other is constitutive. In the political community, the eschatological intersects with time, but for

---

[80] D. WALSH, *The Priority of the Person*, University of Notre Dame, 208.

[81] Ibid., 21.

[82] Ibid., 201-202.

the community to fully function, the citizen needs to live in the realm of responsibility, beyond his or her self. The Church similarly refuses to acknowledge its present institutionalization as its truth in the same way that philosophy stands always within politics, or within the concrete community, but is never determined by it. We are thus able to conclude that as philosophy uncovers what politics can never provide, so theology uncovers what philosophy can never provide.[83]

## 3.11 Balthasar and Walsh: Theology meets Philosophy

Australian Catholic priest Jerome Santamaria masterfully connects Walsh's understanding of personhood with that of the theologian Hans Urs Von Balthasar.[84] In his *The Lord is Here and I did not Know it* (2022), a doctoral dissertation at the Pontifical Gregorian University in Rome, Italy, Santamaria makes the argument that the self-giving of persons, one to the other, is the fundamental category for analyzing not only the agent of, but also the content of the mode of transmission of Revelation. Santamaria observes that as a person is understood as one who gives himself or herself away, according to Walsh, for the sake of other the person, that this dynamic is revealed

[83] Ibid., 208-210.

[84] Cf. J. SANTAMARIA, *The Lord is Here and I did Not Know It: The Revelation of the Person and the Person as Revelatory in the Walsh and Balthasar*, Pontifical Gregorian University, *Tesi Gregoriana*, Rome, *Serie Teologia*, 2022.

definitively in the Eucharist. Santamaria's project[85] reflects on how the Swiss theologian and Walsh both have placed the person as central to their work. For Walsh, Santamaria states, it is by the very nature of the person that Revelation is allowed to occur.[86] Santamaria captures that for Walsh personal language, as opposed to impersonal language, the movement of transcendence, the Incarnation, the mutuality of persons, and God himself as personal, are all characteristic contributions of Walsh's thought.

Regarding Balthasar, Santamaria states that Balthasar does "make something" of the back and forth between self-appropriation and communication, between the inner and external word, but Walsh, he states, moves further insofar as he makes this dynamic constitutive.[87] Santamaria concludes his dissertation by describing the personal manner in which Revelation is received by the person both in Sacred Scripture and in the Holy Eucharist.[88]

As Santamaria places Balthasar and Walsh in dialogue, as we have also attempted to do, albeit to a much lesser extent in this project, David Walsh's philosophy of the person becomes interactive with a rich, Christological and dialogically based theology in Balthasar. Both thinkers contribute from the perspective of different disciplines how one may come to understand the human person as a recipient of Divine Revelation. We therefore share with Santamaria the same desire to plumb the depths of the deeply personal structure and nature of Revelation, and Walsh's work on the person is

---

[85] Ibid., 230-269.

[86] Ibid., 185.

[87] Ibid., 187.

[88] Ibid., 12-20.

truly the context for this mining, as we share the same sentiments that pushed Santamaria to engage Walsh with one of the greatest theologians of the 20th century, and one that was very well versed in dialogical philosophy, Hans urs Von Balthasar.

As we discussed in Part One Chapter One, Balthasar, founded in a rich Christology, understands with Walsh the need to fight against the limits of the subject-object dichotomy. Both the philosopher and the theologian see the importance of subjectivity, and both value the importance of objective truth. Walsh sees the person everywhere, in science, politics, history and art, with Balthasar approaching personhood with the same depth, with the Person of Christ being theologically Concrete and Universal. There is so much more to discover here, when we begin to relate Walsh's contribution ever more deeply with theology, as perhaps our extension of that to Ratzinger, Zizioulas, Maximus, and Betz is but a small contribution in this regard. So much more illumination is yet to even be discovered, as we continue the inexorable search both philosophically and theologically.

## 3.12 Conclusion

In Walsh's *The Priority of the Person: Political, Philosophical and Historical Discoveries* (2020) the political philosopher reminds us that all that is meaningful in our lives flows from persons whom we know and love.[89] With a tinge of a reminiscence of Derrida, the language that we use in our attempts to master the world is humbled and essentially defeated in the encounter with persons who come to

[89] D. WALSH, *Priority of the Person*, 86.

master us. Walsh observes that we can never master or control a person, but they do master us. The thou with whom I speak, and the who that addresses me, is indeed a *who* and not a *what*. Walsh recalls here again that the modern philosophical search inexorably points toward the person as a whole. History is the apocalypse of the person, and modernity enables the moment of its realization. Each person is prior to all else that is, and the person is the pivot around whom everything else revolves, thus making personhood the inexhaustible pivot of all things.

The Jewish Martin Buber (1878-1965) initiated the radical decentering of the self, and this work culminates in Levinas where we find the priority of the other over oneself. Walsh's reappropriation of Kant in a more positive light, due to the latter's prioritization of practical reason over theoretical reason, has reached its denouement, according to Walsh, in the prioritization of the person, in his or her, concrete existence, over all other considerations. *Dasein* for Heidegger is that which holds itself apart from being, and by this, Walsh concludes, the former intended the person. Persons are ends in themselves, beyond the whole. Rights are transcendent when they are approached from the perspective of community, as we all become implicated in the rights of others in the political community.[90]

The political community for Walsh, and we include the Church, must recognize that each of its members is an inexhaustible center of meaning and value. For Levinas, in the face of the other we see most clearly who we are. For Kierkegaard, the individual exceeds the

---

[90] Ibid., 155-179.

universal.[91] The Scholastic theologians and philosophers by no means lacked an interior life, but they could not readily connect it with the form of disputation that their thinking had assumed. Walsh acknowledges that the necessity of saying that the person is "beyond being" seems contrary to all of our established conventions of metaphysics. The Annunciation of the Archangel Gabriel to Mary, however, manifests to us how Revelation occurs only when it is glimpsed through the self-revelation of the other; in this case the Archangel Gabriel to Mary. Every person is unique, irreplaceable, knowable, and incommunicable in his or her self in relation to the other.[92] With David Walsh's recently published book, *The Invisible Source of Authority: God in a Secular Age* (2025), he continues the search, leading us deeper and deeper into the inexplicable mystery of personhood, and the transcendence sourced in God.

---

[91] Ibid., 221-233.

[92] Ibid., 219.

# Chapter Four

# Professor John Betz: A Metaphysical Expansion through Trinitarian Analogy

"There the angel of the Lord appeared to him as fire flaming out of bush. When he looked although the bush was on fire, it was not being consumed."

(Exodus 3:2)

## 4.1 A Theological Methodology

Of great urgency to the theology of today is for the Trinity itself to be understood as the source and origin of Tradition. With the significant theological development of understanding Revelation from a relational perspective, which is in our opinion the imperative issued forth by the Second Vatican Council in *Dei Verbum*, a theological methodology which is more relational provides the opportunity for a rediscovery of Tradition as fundamentally Trinitarian. The 20th Century theological movement of renewal, *Ressourcement*, which pioneered these same objectives, recently emerged anew for reconsideration in Bishop Robert Barron's new theological journal, *The New Ressourcement* of Word on Fire Academic. This occurrence we believe has opened up the doors again to a Trinitarian-based renewal in Western Catholic theology. Betz's lead article in this new academic journal synthesized his thought and is entitled *The Analogy of Tradition: Toward a More Radical Ressourcement.*[1]

Prior to the emergence of this new academic journal, new currents in metaphysics were more limited and restricted to particular schools of theology, such as the Post-Conciliar movement, *Communio*, to which Ratzinger and Balthasar would have largely contributed. Within the first issues of *The New Ressourcement*, a significant theological discussion emerged, which we believe signifies a metaphysical development in mainstream Thomistic theology as discovered in the project of theologian John Betz. Our desire here is to take advantage of this methodological opening provided by Betz. Our intention here is to take advantage of this methodological opening provided by Betz to promote the political philosophy of Professor Walsh, who has been contributing to the understanding of personhood from a philosophical standpoint, but has not yet reached a wider audience in the theological world because of a more constricted and limited metaphysical system that we argue has not been capable of meeting the development of personalism in the Pontificates of Pope Benedict XVI and Pope Francis. Furthermore, our current Western metaphysical system has not been able to adequately capture or appreciate the great contribution that these Popes have made toward the appreciation of the centrality of personhood.

[1] J.R. BETZ, *The Analogy of Tradition: Toward a More Radical Ressourcement*, The New Ressourcement, Word on Fire Academic Journal,. V. 1, n.3, 2024, 535.

In his most recent book, *Christ the Logos of Creation: An Essay in Analogical Metaphysics* (2023), the book from which the lead article in *The New Ressourcement* is derived, Professor Betz introduces a theological methodology that is conducive to our project because it is a metaphysic that is fundamentally Trinitarian and opens up the discipline of metaphysics to a greater appreciation of personhood and relationality. This latest book is published within the *Renewal within Tradition* of Emmaus Academic with Professor Matthew Levering as Editor and seeks to unite the theology of Saint Thomas with theological renewal. In the same lead article mentioned above, as well as in his book, Betz makes the compelling argument for the Trinitarian criterion for an understanding of Tradition as living. He argues that the original Tradition is rooted in the divine nature of the Father as handed over to the Son. This in turn becomes the primary analogate for all theological methodology. This brings Tradition into the relief of primarily addressing the fundamental questions posed by both anthropology and ontology, and opens the door to a more principal understanding of Tradition which carries with it a more adequately relational importance.

## 4.2 Tradition as Trinitarian

For Betz, Tradition begins in the atemporal immanent Trinity. He argues that a weakness in the method of theological traditionalists is that they do not go all of the way back to God Himself, specifically the atemporal Trinity, when thinking about Tradition, but, on the contrary, begin by thinking about Tradition at some later point in ecclesial history. This is most appealing to our project because the immanent Trinity is both dynamic and relational, thus not enabling the primary analogate for Tradition to be objectified by things defined by nature, but rather only by the Trinitarian God Himself. This removes the subjective choice of the theological traditionalist to begin with a certain historical point within Tradition, such as the history of Israel, or even more recently a Patristic or Medieval point of departure. As Tradition, according to Betz, begins with this handing over (*paradosis*) of the divine nature to the Son from the Father, it enables the ontology of human personhood to be rooted in the immanent life of the Holy Trinity. If the language of substance is to be used, then the substance to which the human person is destined is the substance of the Second Person of the Holy Trinity, the eternal *Logos*, Jesus Christ, who shares in the same divine substance as the Father, thus linking the term substance to its divine origin, and removing its philosophical ambiguity.

This argument not only provides an ontological foundation for this our third project, but also for our understanding of Tradition in its entirety, and how it applies to our understanding of the human person. The most radical return to Tradition must be fundamentally rooted in the eternal Trinity. Without this re-orientation of our fundamental understanding of Tradition, our project would not be placed on an adequate metaphysical foundation. Historical and Ecclesial Tradition is only authentic to the extent that it communicates this original Tradition, which is the Father handing over the divine nature to the Son, inspiring persons with the love that the Father has for each of them personally in the Son. We thus come to see in this Tradition not only the origin and the end of all traditions, but also the ultimate criteria which immediately relativizes all other traditions and also provides the criterion for their authenticity.[2]

As the first *Ressourcement* of Catholic theology in the 20th Century, pioneered by great theologians such as Jean Cardinal Danielou, Henri Cardinal de Lubac, and Hans Urs von Balthasar, was a return to the sources, in a search for theology to meet the deeper questions of ontology and anthropology, what is needed now, argues Betz, is the need for an even more radical *Ressourcement*, that is even more adventurous and ecumenical in its return to the sources than the first *Ressourcement*; confident that in the end all things good, true and beautiful in one way or another, by analogy, bear witness to Christ. Rooting his argument in Balthasar's understanding of Tradition, Betz reaffirms the primary sense of tradition; that the Father gives the whole of his nature to the Son and through the Son to each of us, in order that sharing in the same nature as the Son, we may each be made participants in the divine nature. To be a participant in the original Tradition, Betz argues, citing Balthasar, is to be a recipient, the person that is, of the original Tradition, and this is received within the ecclesial body of the Church.

## 4.3 Analogical Metaphysics and Trinitarian Theology

Tradition must be capable at its origin of addressing the most fundamental questions of both ontology and anthropology. Within

---

[2] J.R. BETZ, *Christ the Logos of Creation: An Essay in Analogical Metaphysics*, Emmaus Academic, 2023, 587.

the discipline of Fundamental Theology, Obediential Potency is a Thomistic concept which refers to the capacity of a creature to both receive and be acted upon by God, in a manner which exceeds natural capabilities. It is the intrinsic openness, despite sin, of a person to the supernatural influence and action of God. For Betz, being and consciousness are both obediential potencies that bear a Mariological form and are therefore in their essence open to God, as both of these faculties are analogues of the God who is analogically imaged in them as transcending them.[3] While the person is on the spiritual journey toward God, for Saint Thomas Aquinas and for Medieval theologians in general, Betz states, all of creation remains a similitude, some kind of likeness, but God always will elude the grasp of the person. Betz argues that the traditional understanding of the analogy of being (*analogia entis*) is the fundamental form, or the dynamic transcendence, and applies beyond natural theology even to the greatest and most supernatural revelations.[4] The essential meaning of the *meta* in metaphysics as the transcendence of the thing in itself toward another, defines the precise meaning of the formality of analogy.[5]

A perennial philosophical problem, which Betz's project hopes to assist in correcting, is in the absolutization of essence (thought)[6] in various forms of idealism, and on the other hand the problem of absolutizing existence (being) in various forms of realism. Citing Kierkegaard, Betz makes the argument that thought, or essence,

---

[3] Ibid., 86.

[4] Ibid., 93.

[5] Ibid., 128.

[6] Ibid., 134.

must always be connected with life,[7] and in doing so he implicitly concurs with both Professor Walsh and Metropolitan Zizioulas. In fact, we will advance the same argument in Part Three of this project with Zizioulas. We thus find here in the work of Betz, a solidification of these principles, being solidified in a Western theological context, on the shoulders of great theologians such as David Schindler and Tracey Rowland, who have preceded Betz in the interpretation of Saint Thomas, along with the appreciation of the limitations present within his thought. As Saint Thomas teaches clearly that theology does not destroy nature but rather perfects it (*theologia non destruit sed supponit et perficit philosophiam*), we may truly come to understand that not only are philosophy and theology analogically related, but that they are so profoundly interrelated that they penetrate each other not in a confused way, but in a manner that each becomes itself, as it were, and its peculiar lineaments begin to stand out, only in analogical relation to one another.[8] This discovery of Betz, that faith essentially may be dependent on reason for deeper elucidation, will enable us not only to use analogy to describe the relationship of the human person to God, but also the philosophical concept of *metaxy*, a term which we will be define below. We may thus rightly conclude with Betz that the relationship between analogical metaphysics and Trinitarian theology is demanded on the principle of the relationship between reason and faith. Yet, we cannot rely on Saint Thomas alone, because of the pervading problem of postmodern

---

[7] Ibid.

[8] Ibid., 165. Here Betz refers to the theological contribution of Emmanuel Falque of the *Institute Catholique de Paris*, on this topic.

unbelief.[9] Betz, similarly to Australian theologian Tracey Rowland, relies on a Catholic theological method that must include an interplay between Saint Thomas and Saint Augustine,[10] whereas in our project we use the fundamental principles established and emphasized by Betz and apply the principles more broadly, particularly to Saint Maximus the Confessor (Part Three, Chapter Five) and Metropolitan John Zizioulas (Part Three, Chapters Six through Eight).

## 4.4 The Human Person as *Tamquam Ignotus*

Seen from this perspective, Betz states, drawing from the great the German Jesuit philosopher and theologian Erich Przywara, (1889-1972) whose understanding of analogy of being had a fundamental influence on Balthasar, the human person is that which is never completed, as the human person always remains the inconclusive openness of its tensions. The *maior dissimultudo*[11] of the Fourth Lateran Council, which doctrinally confirms that God always exceeds to that which he is compared, we argue may be applied analogically to the human person, and if so situated, places the human person on the trajectory of being undefinable, insofar as he or she by analogy is compared with the ineffability of God. In consonance with Professor Walsh, the human person is beyond being, and must therefore be defined by something beyond nature, and if the person

---

[9] Ibid., 166.

[10] T. ROWLAND, *Culture and the Thomist Tradition After Vatican II*, Routledge Radical Orthodoxy, 2003.

[11] Ibid., 92.

is defined by God, the person will always exceed definition by analogy to God.

Betz, citing Przywara's reference to Saint Thomas Aquinas indeed that as God remains *tamquam ignotus*, beyond all conceivable contents,[12] that the human person by analogy may also be understood, in our opinion, to remain similar. This provides a context, in our opinion, for the human person to be understood in the context of a Tradition that is fundamentally Trinitarian, and locates the human person in the eternal flowing forth of the Son from the Father.[13] If God is incomprehensible, even to the person of faith,[14] to ground our understanding of personhood in reason alone, would be like trying to ground a flowing river in its flowing.[15]

Betz describes analogy as looking more like a dynamic, rhythmic, tensile oscillation between alternative standpoints, such that each is secretly "in" the other, as "other" to the other.[16] Finite being is not self-enclosed, or explicable in its own terms, and must be understood according to analogy as the rhythmic form of thought, and not by logic alone. Analogy thus enables the mystery of the human

---

[12] Ibid.

[13] J.R. BETZ, *The Analogy of Tradition: Towards a More Radical Ressourcement, New Ressourcement*, V. 1, n.3, 2024, 535.

[14] J.R. BETZ, *Christ the Logos of Creation*, 115.

[15] Ibid., 126. See also T. ROWLAND, *Culture and the Thomist Tradition after Vatican II*, Routledge, 2003, for a similar critical analysis of some of deficiencies in a purely Thomistic methodology in addressing the modern epistemological and cultural problems.

[16] Ibid., 130.

person to be expressed in a manner that eludes definition.[17] This leads to an understanding of the person as a secondary procession through the Son, which is analogous to the first procession of the Son from the Father.[18]

Furthermore, Betz states that it is reasonable to argue in a speculative manner that the very shape of knowledge is Trinitarian.[19] To therefore locate an understanding of the human person in the eternal procession of the Son from the Father in the atemporal immanent Trinity is indeed a speculative possibility in the realm of theology, which thus may affect our understanding of person philosophically as well; notably through the concept of *metaxis* accompanying analogy, as metaxy's reference point is merely transcendental, which may serve either to broaden our understanding of participation in the Holy Trinity by way of philosophy, or to locate the human person more specifically in that secondary procession of the Son from the Father which is eternal and ongoing. As analogy eludes definition, its primary analogate is the Trinity in classical Catholic theology and metaphysics, *metaxy* may have an even greater capacity to elude definition, in our opinion, as the general "in-betweenness" between the divine and the human that it represents may serve as a gateway for philosophy to enter into theology, or as a manner to describe Trinitarian participation more loosely and freely so as to engage a less Trinitarian oriented seeker.

---

[17] Cf Ibid., 131 regarding German Jesuit priest Erich Przywara S.J.'s (1889-1972) presentation of analogy.

[18] Ibid., 140.

[19] Ibid., 141.

## 4.5 Beyond Ipsum Esse Subsistens

If God is understood as being itself in the West, it is imperative that this being must be understood as a mystery, and that there subsequently may be a link to personhood, according to Betz as he brilliantly argues that it will not be sufficient for Christian metaphysics simply to say that God IS, that God is being, or as Saint Thomas himself defines that God is *ipsum esse subsistens* (the subsistent being itself). This limited meaning, only stating that God is being, emphasizes that essence and existence coincide only in God, as this is ordinally a terminal statement, thus not extending to how it may affect the human person in his or her self. While this principle is metaphysically true, we must also posit simultaneously that creatures, or the human person, are always becoming who they are called to be. There must be a movement beyond the sheer act of being itself, into personhood, something beyond this Western understanding of God's being which no longer shackles our understanding of existence in the context of personhood only by way of a *via negativa*; that is by stating what existence cannot be. For the West, therefore, God is being itself, but is beyond being identified by a *genus*, so beyond *genus*.

Walsh, however, makes the bold step beyond by stating that the human person stands outside of being, indeed beyond being. This places Walsh outside the traditional Aristotelian and Thomistic metaphysical structure, and therefore unites him with Betz in stating that the understanding of *ipsum esse subsistens*, while true, is not enough for the development of personhood. "Beyond" is an adverb in this regard which always points to being "beyond substance" (not identified by *genus*) and thus beyond "full comprehension" (*tamquam ignotus*), and in this instance of the definition of *ipse esse subsistens,* we must heed the call to go beyond of Walsh and Betz into the realm of mystery beyond being for personhood.

The human person, and indeed all of creation which is sensibly perceived, does not actually subsist, but only the transcendent essence, on which everything else depends, alone subsists.[20] This thinking should do no less than plunge us into the mystery of the human person as a dynamic becoming, but ontologically dependent on something outside of oneself, mainly the subsistence of the Creator, on which all being and personhood are dependent. What better place for this ontological dependence to be realized than in the event of the Holy Eucharist, where the person is being regularly transformed in an ontological manner. The human person is dependent upon the Holy Eucharist, because realities which do not derive their being from themselves, but from someone else, do not really exist as the divine persons of the Holy Trinity do, but they rather *in-sist*, insofar as they subsist in something else. Betz thus argues that the persons of the Trinity inform us of what it means to exist, in the original and primary sense of the word, by analogy,[21] thus pointing us toward the relational ontological reality of personhood.

---

[20] Ibid., 179. Here Betz refers to Gregory of Nyssa (335-394) and his *The Life of Moses.*

[21] Ibid., 181. Here Betz refers to Richard of St. Victor's (1110-1173) *De Trinitate.*

## 4.6 Metaxological Betweening

All created persons are analogues of God, and God is the source of their analogical reality. The analogue for the begetting of persons is the eternal self-giving of the Father. In fact, according to Professor Betz, all of creation may be understood according to a secondary procession of the Son from the Father. Betz argues that love is the meaning of being from the beginning, and that being by way of analogy is love.[22] By way of love, we pierce the mysteries of things, and only through love is epistemology possible. For Betz, the primary analogate must be love, and the philosophical concept of *metaxy*, in perhaps a greater manner than analogy, will be able to illustrate love theologically because the term is more dynamic and flexible, while at the same time applying to a wider philosophical audience. This *metaxy* is a philosophical concept for describing the in-betweenness of the divine and the human. Analogy necessarily involves *cataphatic* descriptions of the similarities between the divine and human. But, there are contents of Revelation of the Godhead that are beyond the cataphatic but which we understand and can relate to in a certain sense. For example, God dying on the cross is not able to be described by analogy and, in fact, confounds all analogy. This means that the cataphatic descriptions are alone insufficient to describe our relationship and participation in God. Thus, the philosophical concept of *metaxy* opens up an *apophatic* dimension that describes the indescribable aspects of our relationship with God.

---

[22] J.R. BETZ, *Christ the Logos of Creation*, 233-241.

*Metaxy*, with its Platonic origins, may therefore, as described earlier, philosophically serve to assist in understanding how love is illumined in nature, reflecting its mysterious dynamism and flexibility in a less precise manner according to the primary analogate of transcendence.

For example, William Desmond, in his reflection of the contribution of Betz in relationship to his thinking on the indispensability of analogy, gives a substantial contribution to the role of the figurative insofar as it pertains to the recuperation of contemplation. Desmond describes his own understanding of the analogy of being, following the foundational thought of Plato and, much later, of Eric Voegelin as a "metaxological betweening."[23] Desmond, along with Betz, understands that Martin Heidegger has exercised an incredible influence on the discourse of metaphysics in the 20th century, and into our own time, so one manner of adequately addressing his questions is through the use of *metaxy*.[24] Furthermore, Desmond astutely notes that the neglect of the metaphysical in contemporary philosophy is due to the prioritization of the practical over the theoretical, a good philosophical intuition, but with consequences. *Metaxy* thus serves as a way to philosophically open the door to that which is beyond being, which actually may serve to describe "betweenings" in a manner and to an audience that Trinitarian analogy is not capable of reaching or describing. As described above, *Metaxy* may therefore serve as a philosophical entry into participation in God, but in

[23] W. DESMOND, *Analogy, Agape, and Metaxological Metaphysics*, New Ressourcement, V. 1, #4, Winter 2024, 869.

[24] Ibid., 870.

a manner that is even more contemplative, mysterious, flexible, and most importantly dynamic, serving as a handmaid to Trinitarian analogy. For example, we have truly witnessed how contemplation leads one into this "betweening" of God and the human person.

While our project argues that the contemporary desire for the practical, or the ethical, should be a point of departure, which must be embraced in order to dialogue with contemporary philosophy, we at the same time have arrived at the understanding that the contemporary philosopher, while neglecting metaphysics, at the same time possesses an *incognito* metaphysics.[25] *Metaxy* opens the human person to the mystery of deeper thinking and prayer that overcomes the ethos of serviceable disposability, and the predominance of a calculative sense of thinking that leads to the tragic loss of contemplation, so necessary for Christianity, as it appreciates being or beauty for the sake of itself,[26] and as a vessel that leads the mind to God. Metaphysics, Desmond warns, could come to be neglected or forgotten.[27] He astutely warns that the contemporary person is even more privy to a technological tyranny that isolates and drives own toward isolation, with social media becoming a mask that features itself as communal, but really only serves as a false form of the communal, leading to an absence of contemplation and thus to isolation.

---

[25] Ibid, 871.

[26] Ibid, 872.

[27] Ibid, 872. David Schindler also makes a similar argument to the one of Desmond in his theological project. Cf. D.L. SCHINDLER, *Heart of the World Center of the Church: Communio, Ecclesiology, Liberalism, and Liberation*, Eerdmans, 1996.

Overcoming a technological and overly analytical mindset is central to this project, because we have come to see how it reduces the potential of personhood as dynamically unfolding in the mystery of the otherness of God. Desmond supports this line of thinking by understanding that metaphysics carries an *incarnational* character which must companion the figurative in the highest and best of its thoughts.[28] More metaphysical and theological imagination is needed, Desmond argues, so as to reach out to earlier companions, such as the modern philosophers, in the search for truth. With Betz, Desmond argues, the metaphysical and the theological are actualized by the analogical.[29] Betz's contribution, based on the thought of Erich Przywara, offers an understanding of analogy not rooted in a static structure of relations, but rather as a dynamic happening of relating with an immense suppleness to understand nuances of "betweenings" as modes of relating.[30] Desmond remarkably notes that this "betweening" is first seen in the relationships of God in the Holy Trinity, between God in relation to his beloved creation, as well as between Jesus in the mystery of His Incarnation and his divine companioning with his beloved creature,[31] as well as the human person on an active journey of discipleship. According to Desmond, if "betweening" is able to describe the relations within the Trinity, wherein we witness its theological application, thus illustrating its vast range and capacity, then why would that same suppleness and

---

[28] W. DESMOND, *Analogy, Agape and Metaxological Metaphysics*, 875.

[29] Ibid, 876.

[30] Ibid, 879.

[31] Ibid, 879.

nuance of inter-Trinitarian relations not also be extended to the relationship between the divine and the human? If love is the meaning of being, both analogy and *metaxy* will each describe the richness and uniqueness of this kind of relating. *Metaxy* may thus serve to take us more into the beyond theologically, beyond the traditional confines of analogy, by way of a stretching, and it dynamically serves as a handmaid to analogy.

## 4.7 *Analogia Caritatis*

Furthering this metaphysical and analogical stretching, Betz indeed concludes that Christ on the Cross discloses that the relation of other to other is so complete in the person of Christ that divinity indeed gives itself up for humanity, and humanity in turn gives itself up for divinity. He describes this divine exchange so perfectly by stating that "the one others itself into the other for the sake of the other," thereby perfecting the *analogia entis* by the love of God in Christ.[32] Betz then concludes that the original integrity of the *analogia entis* reappears in the event of the Cross as the *analogia caritatis.*[33] Masterfully then Betz then describes how the *maior dissimultudo* (God is always greater than the human person may understand) of the Fourth Lateran Council, now in the event of the Cross becomes a theological Revelation of the depths of God's love for human beings. The concept of *analogia entis* may no longer be defined by the perennial philosophical search from below

[32] J.R. BETZ, *Christ the Logos of Creation*, 227.

[33] Ibid.

(cataphatic) by inference, but now, after the event of the Cross, only by the greatness of God in the form of an ever greater love.[34] Betz describes the death of God on the Cross as being utterly unintelligible to classical metaphysics, and so the event of the Cross marks a kind of death for classical metaphysics as well. Being is seen to become nothing on the Cross. Now, Betz argues, we have a new metaphysics that embraces *nothing*, and even becomes *nothing*, in order that *nothing* might Be. We now must cling to the Cross to understand Being, as Being cannot be understood apart from the Cross.[35]

Desmond, following Betz, astutely observes, and following his own methodology, and states that being on the Cross is a "metaxological betweening" of both divine abjectness and divine glory.[36] He states that what was at issue is both being and love, God being love. We must now come to see that being is love, and love is being. "Love is the being of God; God is the being of love." Desmond, building on the contribution of Betz, describes this self-affirming love of God to Godself with the beautiful divine term of "agapeic betweening."[37] Desmond then concludes by adding the importance of self-love to the other kinds of love, stating that if God is *agape*, then this must be a love that loves itself also, its own being itself, this being love and nothing but love. The person thus finds the affirmation of his or her own being at work in his or her own being, the self-affirmation of

---

[34] Ibid, 228. Here Betz cites the work of Erich Przywara.

[35] Ibid.

[36] W. DESMOND, *Analogy, Agape, and Metaxological Metaphysics*, 886.

[37] Ibid., 888.

each individual person, always understood as part of the collective we in the one Christ of love.[38]

Finally, we taste and see the opening of the doors of a Western understanding of metaphysics that begs the assistance of the Eastern lung of the Catholic Church. For to follow these methodological lines in their depth, one must turn to a cosmological metaphysics that is at the same time faithful to the order of nature but not shackled by its limitations.

---

[38] Ibid., 887.

# PART THREE

## *PROPOSALS*

## *METAPHYSICAL AND THEOLOGICAL PROPOSALS*

# Chapter Five

# Maximus the Confessor: An Eastern Patristic Metaphysical Foundation

"Before I formed you in the womb I knew you." (Jeremiah 1:5)

## 5.1 A Cosmic Vision

Following Origen and Pseudo-Dionysius the Areopagite, Maximus the Confessor serves not only as the Patristic bridge between the East and the West, but he also provides a metaphysical foundation for understanding the priority of the personal in salvation.[1] For Maximus, God stands beyond being,[2] which in the first instance draws us to his contribution because of how it theologically responds to our questions, providing the foundation for an adequate metaphysic. Our second project, *Personhood and Communion* (2018) was directed by a scholar of Saint Maximus the Confessor from the Faculty of the Pontifical Gregorian University in Rome, Italy, the German Reverend Philipp Renczes, S.J.[3] Renczes studied

[1] See A. RIOU, *Le Monde Et L'Église Selon Maxime Le Confesseur*, Paris, 1973, 86-87 for an argument that the personal, or hypostatic order, has a priority in the initiative of salvation.

[2] H. U. BALTHASAR, *Cosmic Liturgy: The Universe According to Maximus the Confessor*, Ignatius, San Francisco, CA, 2003, 217.

[3] P.G. RENCZES, S.J. has also served as the Dean of the Faculty of Theology and Director of the Department of Patristic Theology at the

Maximus at the Sorbonne (University of Paris). It was in studying for the doctorate under Renczes that we came to appreciate ever more deeply a vision of grace in more personalist terms. We therefore began under his direction the initial exploration for our second project of a broader metaphysical foundation based in the relation of the whole of creation to the Trinity and the Eucharistic Liturgy. Renczes helped us discover that our project must be rooted in a Patristic source, and in Renczes we found a professor who lamented the detachment of the theology in the West from Eastern sources after the Council of Trent. He confirmed for us that a weakness in the contribution of Saint Thomas Aquinas was that he explains the parts better than he explains the whole, and that he was aware of the unified vision, and tried to explain it with all of the precisions, but became too substance based and not enough personalistic. To this point, for example, Hans Urs Von Balthasar credits Maximus the Confessor for the understanding that God is not *ousia*, but that he stands over and above *ousia*.[4] Furthermore, Balthasar is drawn to the fact that Maximus always refers back to the relational term *hypostasis*[5] when speaking about nature, as the former seems to

Pontifical Gregorian University, as well as Full Professor of Dogmatic Theology of the same University. Furthermore, he has served as invited Professor at the Pontifical Oriental Institute at the same Pontifical Gregorian University and an invited Professor at the Patristic Institute *Augustinianum* in Rome, Italy. He also occupied the Wade Chair at Marquette University Milwaukee, USA in 2007.

[4] H. U. BALTHASAR, *Cosmic Liturgy: The Universe According to Maximus the Confessor*, 217. This text reveals Balthasar's discovery of Maximus.

[5] Cf. H.U. BALTHASAR, *Cosmic Liturgy*, 223.

connect with the latter in the inherent understanding that nature is insufficient alone to understand the mystery of personhood.

The rich theological contribution to anthropology in Maximus is situated within the context of a grand ontological vision of being. For Maximus, being is understood from three perspectives: Dynamic, Analogical, and Finality. The dynamic nature of being includes the vision of God, which for Maximus is clearly distinct from Platonism, because for Maximus being does not originate in pre-existent matter. Regarding finality, being has its beginning in God, and its end in God. The human person, for Maximus, is thus being in all of its totality, and includes the end of the human person, his or her finality.

The Eastern philosophical historian Endre Von Ivanka (1902-1974), credits Maximus with appreciating and responding to both the Aristotelian and Platonic questions regarding being, somehow within the context of the mystery of the illumination of the theological upon the natural in the search for the meaning of personhood. Von Ivanka finds that there is a synthesis achieved by Maximus that achieves a unity in the thought between the two great Greek philosophers of Plato and Aristotle, yet at the same time is free of dualism (Plato) and immanentism (Aristotle).[6] Perennially, Greek philosophy from the very beginning was marked by attempts to understand the relationship between the human and the divine, and Maximus masterfully achieves the answer to the question that both of the great philosophers have asked, yet at the same time is providentially not

---

[6] E. VON IVANKA, *Maximus the Confessor: All in One In Christ*, Johannes Verlag, 1961, 232,233.

influenced by either of them, because the Holy Spirit is his ultimate teacher and guide.

Even today, our understanding of God is both immanent (*cataphatic*), as we experience God, and also always at the same time radically transcendent and *apophatic*, leading the human person to surrender to the great mystery of God that cannot be contained in words. Essentially, to a mystic, God can seem so close, yet at the same time so far away.

## 5.2 Dynamic Being

One cannot begin to appreciate an ontology of being in theology without first appreciating the contribution of the Church Father Origen of Alexandria (185-254). Origin's *De Principis* (On First Principles) is an interdisciplinary work, combining both Christian and philosophical elements.[7] From Origen, it becomes evident for the first time that in the order of Christian Revelation we must both have 1) changing being and 2) that the human person is defined by this ontological mode of changing being.[8] The point of departure in the order of movement for Origen is first 1) *stasis* (rest); then *genesis* (creation); and finally *kinesis* (motion).

For Maximus, the point of departure in the order of movement begins in Salvation History with the real and practical situation of the fallen human person placed within an inherently good creation,

---

[7] E. VON IVANKA, *Plato Christianus*, Johannes Verlag, Einsiedeln, 1964, 95.

[8] U. BIANCHI, "Platonic Presuppositions," in *Selected Essays on Gnosticism, Dualism, and Mysteriosophy*, Brill Academic, 1978, 45-49.

*genesis* (creation), followed by *kinesis* (movement), and ending with *stasis* (rest).[9] Notice how Christian metaphysics for Maximus begins with Salvation History, thus the practical place where the human person finds his or her self, beginning with the concrete and real, in a concrete time and place of history. Movement then leads to a superior level of grace for Maximus through Redemption, and subsequent Divinization.[10]

There is something which very much distinguishes the Christian ontology of Maximus from traditional Greek ontology, and the latter's *monistic* structure, wherein there was no distinction between the created and the uncreated realm. The movement of the created order is thus metaphysically something good and proper to the order. For Maximus, the dynamic nature of being is understood in the context of both analogy and finality. Pertaining to finality, being has its beginning in God, and its end in God. In this context, one can find in Maximus that the human person is actually being in all of its totality. This realization was an achievement that Scholastic philosophy was not able to as clearly achieve, and is most pressing for the existential questions of our present day. The finality of the human person is carried within the person as the person chooses and moves through time through ethical choices in Christ the *Logos.* Analogy thus become the link, as developed by Professor Betz in Chapter Three, and becomes the very context in which the human person is plunged into divinization, and this is achieved in the metaphysics of Maximus only by finality, or eschatology, that which we will be in

---

[9] P.G. RENCZES, S.J., "Philosophical Anthropology of Maximus," 62.
[10] Ibid.

the future, and are becoming now through grace, to inform nature. This essential dimension of finality in metaphysics, coupled with movement, must have theological eschatology as its governing principle, and within history we will find that this eschatology is fully realized in the celebration of the Holy Eucharist.

Accepting both the fact that being is always in movement, and that it also bears truth, it must be understood as drawing its meaning from the future, from the eschatological, and not from nature in itself. Nature, insofar as it is subject to death and decay, is not capable of giving truth to being. It may be proposed that a being, because it is historical, and therefore necessarily dynamic, receives its animation from the one *Logos*, toward which it is moving. Based in this principle of the *Logos* and the *logoi*, if a being is going to be, it must be in God.[11] If the dynamism of creation is animated by the one *Logos*, then it may be concluded that not only the dynamism of the historical is animated by the eschatological, but also that the dynamic nature of being participates in order and in truth.

## 5.3 The Humanization of God and the Divinization of the Person

While at the same time creation is understood as being *ex nihilo*, thus marking the radical distinction between the nature of God and the nature of the human person, with the Father's desire to create the radically other being a product of his loving will, this creation

---

[11] See A. Riou, *Le Monde Et L'Église Selon Maxime Le Confesseur*, 56 for an argument that the *logos/logoi* terminology begins in the Alexandrian tradition.

"out of nothing" leaves the space for an *apophatic* infinite opening between God and humanity, but also the opportunity for great immanence and closeness of God to humanity through the Incarnation. Maximus is able to capture well these two necessary elements of an adequate theological anthropology. This anthropology is best situated within the context of the humanization of God and the divinization of the human person. Both radical immanence and radical transcendence are needed for the complete understanding of the human person being inserted into a mystery where such closeness with God and union with Him is realized, but at the same time He always remains totally other.

Maximus, in his *Ambigua* 7, describes the reciprocal exchange of love between the divine and the human:

> By his gracious condescension God became man and is called man for the sake of man and by exchanging his condition for ours revealed the power that elevates man to God through his love for God and brings God down to man because of his love for man. By this blessed inversion, man is made God by divinization and God is made man by hominization.[12]

For Maximus, grace comes from God, so that the human person may return to God and be in relationship with God. Grace includes all of

---

[12] MAXIMUS THE CONFESSOR, *Ambigua* 7, in *On The Cosmic Mystery of Jesus Christ: Selected Writings from St. Maximus the Confessor*, eds., P. M. Blowers and R.L. Wilken, 60.

the disciplines of theology within itself because it addresses the relationship between God and the human person. It therefore includes theological anthropology, eschatology and ecclesiology, which we argued in the second project must be absolutely considered as Eucharistic. Grace is the participation for the human person in the divine life, divinization, wherein the human person becomes Godlike by grace, not by essence. The humanization of God provides a rich metaphor for what is actually transpiring in the mystery of the Incarnation, and how that effects the relationship of the human person to the Divine Person in Christ.[13]

The Incarnation in Maximus is that it manifests the purpose for which all creatures are given being.[14] The logic of the connection of all created being with the Incarnation may be clearly understood by Maximus here in his *Questiones ad Thallassium* 60:

> This is the great and hidden mystery, at once the blessed end for which all things are ordained. It is the divine purpose conceived before the beginning of created beings. In defining it we would say that this mystery is the preconceived goal for which everything exists, but which itself exists on account of nothing. With a clear view to this end, God created the essences of created beings, and such is, properly speaking, the

---

[13] P.G. RENCZES, S.J., "La Gloria del Padre e la pienezza dell'umano. L'apporto di Massimo Confessore a una precisazione dell'antropologia teologica dei Padri," in L. MELINA , J.J. PEREZ-SOBA (ed)., *Il Bene e la Persona nell'Agire,* Roma, 2002, 147-157, 9.

[14] See A. NICHOLS, O.P., *Byzantine Gospel: Maximus the Confessor in Modern Scholarship*, Edinburgh, 1993, 135-136.

> terminus of his providence and of the things under his providential care. Inasmuch as it leads to God, it is the recapitulation of the things he has created. It is the mystery which circumscribes all the ages, and which reveals the grand plan of God, a super-infinite plan preexisting the ages.[15]

The theology of Maximus the Confessor is therefore realized in the distinction between the absolutely integral human will of Jesus Christ with his divine will, realized in the divinization of the human nature of Jesus Christ.[16] Through this lens we are able to see the unity in the human person of the natural and supernatural because of the grace of participation in the Incarnation. Divinization for Maximus is the redeeming of the will of the human person.[17] Notably, for Maximus, the ability of the human person to become divinized by grace is actualized in the unity of the act of volition, which becomes the unity of divine grace acting upon the choice of the human person. Furthermore, the human person acting in grace is always identified in a state of dynamic movement from the beginning of one's life to the end, and the movement is reflected in the particular moral choices of the human person. Every choice is particular

---

[15] MAXIMUS THE CONFESSOR, *Questiones Ad Thallassium*, 60, in On The Cosmic Mystery of Jesus Christ: Selected Writings from St. Maximus the Confessor, eds., P. M. Blowers and R.L. Wilken, 124-125. See A. RIOU, *Le Monde Et L'Église Selon Maxime Le Confesseur*, 145 for an opinion that Maximus turns away from the neo-platonist cosmological scheme, to the understanding that the Church reorients all things in Christ.

[16] P.G. RENCZES, S.J., "The Gloria del Padre," 8.

[17] Ibid., 7.

and unique to the human person. His anthropological point of departure is creation, followed by movement, and ending in a superior level of grace.[18] Thus movement, and the place of the human will in this movement mark his thought.

## 5.4 Love and Otherness

Maximus identifies the *logoi* as products of the will of the Father. He states, "if God made all things by his will (which no one denies), and it is always pious and right to say that God knows his own will, and that he made each creature by an act of the will, then God knows existing things as he knows the products of his own will."[19] The will of course, in this classically Christian sense, is identified with the love of the Father, and is distinguished from God simply knowing things by their own nature (classically Greek). According to Maximus, God knows things only because he first loves them.

Even in the *eschaton* there is neither absorption nor assimilation of the human into the divine, but otherness is always maintained. In this cosmological dynamic, human freedom, and the infinite particular space for all of the diversity that each person may bring as they

---

[18] P.G. RENCZES, S.J., "The Concept of *hexis* in Theological Anthropology of Saint Maximus the Confessor," in M. VASILJEVIC (ed), *Knowing the Purpose of Creation through the Resurrection*. Proceedings of the Symposium on Saint Maximus the Confessor, Alhambra, CA, 2013, 181-191.

[19] MAXIMUS THE CONFESSOR, *Ambigua* 7, in *On The Cosmic Mystery of Jesus Christ: Selected Writings from St. Maximus the Confessor*, eds., P. M. Blowers, R.L. Wilken, 62. Cf. J. ZIZIOULAS, *Being As Communion*, 97. See A. RIOU, *Le Monde Et L'Église Selon Maxime Le Confesseur*, 47.

proceed in this dramatic movement of motion and dialogue, marks his or her passage in time and place as the human person participates in the divine through moral choices.

With the contribution of Maximus, love is understood as giving rise to otherness, thus giving otherness ontological value, as God is understood as loving something outside and different from himself. Not only is God *ek-static*, but the *logoi* are ordered to be *ek-static* as well,[20] not only in their relation to the *Logos*, but also in their relation to other *logoi*. The freedom of the *logoi* will necessarily be ordered in an interpersonal manner, as each *logoi* must go out to other *logoi* in a manner so as to grow in his or her self-knowledge and awareness and grow in his or her eschatological personhood, analogously to how the *Logos* is relational with the Father. If the person were solely determined by nature, this necessary relationality among the *logoi* for an accretion in being would be regarded as merely accidental in the life of the person, and separated from the divine. Love and otherness, as integral to the ontology and the metaphysics, on the other hand, enable the relational dynamic to be fully integrated and valued.[21] Further to our point regarding relationality, in the *Ambigua* 7, Maximus speaks of contemplation as essential to the process of divinization, and regards it as a form of active receptivity because as one receives power from outside of oneself, one becomes capable, according to Maximus, of generating power that is effective beyond

---

[20] Cf. A. RIOU, *Le Monde Et L'Église Selon Maxime Le Confesseur*, 87. A. NICHOLS, Byzantine Gospel, 133.

[21] See P. SHERWOOD, OSB, "St. Maximus the Confessor", in *Ancient Christian Writers*, eds., J. QUASTEN, J.C. PLUMBE, 31- 32.

oneself.[22] This understanding of reception as act is a necessary and helpful distinction due to the fact that while respecting the dynamic character of being and act, it at the same time proves that receptivity to the other does not threaten the dynamic nature of being and its movement toward perfection, but, to the contrary, it is a proper metaphysical distinction that understands receptivity as necessary for perfection. This is most helpful when it pertains to the attribution of affective qualities and virtues to moral growth.[23]

What we have observed here in this cosmological metaphysics is that it is at the same time a personalist metaphysics because it proceeds from the personal love of the Father. In fact, every particular *logoi* may be identified exclusively with the love of the Father, as each *logoi* was eternally willed by the Father. All of created reality, in its particularity, including the height of creation which is the particularity of the human person, is a product of the will, which is the

---

[22] Cf. MAXIMUS THE CONFESSOR, in *On The Cosmic Mystery of Jesus Christ: Selected Writings from St. Maximus the Confessor*, eds, P. M. BLOWERS, R.L. WILKEN, 64.

[23] See W.R. OXLEY, "An Intimate Gaze: The Father with His Beloved Son the Priest," in *The Priest As Beloved Son*, Institute for Priestly Formation, Omaha, ed. J. KEATING, 2015; and W.R. OXLEY, "Intelligence of the Heart: Rediscovering Relation as a Value in Priestly Formation, in *Seminary Theology III: Seminary Formation and Psychology*, Institute for Priestly Formation, Omaha, Ne, ed. J. KEATING, 2013. With these essays we desired to contribute to the metaphysical appreciation of affectivity and emotion in the life of virtue. For the latter, under the direction of Deacon James Keating of Kenrick Glennon Seminary in Saint Louis, MO, we teamed with Suzanne Baars, daughter of Dr. Conrad Baars, who contributed deeply to the value of affectivity and emotion in the context of personhood.

love, of the Father. We thus find imperative for this project that causality and knowledge, nature and essence, are not in the first instance the most fundamental ontological metaphysic of creation, but rather from a more personalist perspective, love and otherness. The metaphysical contribution of Maximus manifests the ontological value of both love and otherness. Love always gives rise to otherness, which gives the otherness of every particular thing ontological value. With this thoroughly Incarnation based Christian metaphysics, love is the ultimate link between the *Logos* and the *logoi*. This differs radically from Greek thought, where the ultimate link between God was *nous*, or knowledge. Furthermore, because the *Logos*, through which all things are created, and the eschatological Christ, are the same *Logos*, it may be concluded that the *Logos* gives truth to all of created existence. In a Platonic understanding only the original bears the truth, not the future, and the eschatological is precluded from determining the truth of the distinction between the created and the uncreated.

Essentially, based in the Incarnation of the eternal Son of God, with the possession of two wills, as an act of love of the Father, and the Redemption of the human person through the death and Resurrection of Jesus, we are provided with a metaphysic which encompasses the dialogical love story between the divine and the human; which Balthasar describes as a "theandric synergy" of one's existence lived out in its relation with the divine. This not only ontologically affirms the dignity of every human person, but in the celebration of the ontological uniqueness of each person, the incomparable richness of the diversity amongst created persons and all created things is metaphysically appreciated.

## 5.5 The Dyothelite Contribution

Maximus the Confessor refused to accept the heresy of Monothelitism, which denied the existence of a human will in the person of Jesus and was condemned in the definition of the Third Council of Constantinople (680/681) which declared the union of two wills in one person, without separation or division, the human always submitting to the divine.[24] Prior to that, in the year 658, Maximus was brought before the Emperor and Patriarch of Constantinople to be tried as a heretic. Because of his theological position, which was later vindicated at the aforementioned Sixth Ecumenical Council, he at the time had has tongue ripped out and was exiled for preaching this truth.[25] It is evident from this history, that due to this truth confirmed by the Sixth Ecumenical Council, the human person is able to see that their own human will, as united with the human will of Jesus Christ, is able to become divinized without losing any of their integral humanity. Therefore, when the human person is engaged in the moral act of freely choosing, the ontological union with Christ raises this action to a dignity of the same character as it moves towards its own eschatological end, the eternal life of the Holy Trinity, the source from which he or she came. Maximus holds perfectly in tension both obedience and freedom, of both conforming our lives

---

[24] THIRD COUNCIL OF CONSTANTINOPLE, 680/681, DS, #557-558.

[25] J.P. CUSH and W. R. OXLEY, *Theology as Prayer*, 61-62.

to Christ, and at the same time retaining our own identity.[26] Professor Anthony Marco continues:

> The Confessor's thought addresses an underlying problem that vexes our secularized age: the disconnection between faith and life in the world. Two themes are central to this issue: freedom and meaning. First, how does human freedom interact with God's will? Second, does human creativity and meaning-making add to God's plan for creation or are these faculties mere temptations that cause us to stray from the divine will.[27]

With the actions of the human person in movement, and God cooperating with that movement through the grace of the Incarnation is something far greater than a monolithic obedience, but on the other hand the humanization of God opens up infinite and eternal space in the actualization of how human freedom is exercised in relation to God's will.[28] Christ's human will is the hinge upon which the goodness of human freedom depends.[29] The dogmatic truth of Dyothelitism over Monothelitism confirms that human freedom has been totally redeemed, and if human freedom has been redeemed, there is infinite and eternal space within that freedom for self-

---

[26] A. MARCO, "Maximus the Confessor's Answer to the Crisis of Meaning," Church Life Journal, A Journal of the McGrath Institute for Church Life, University of Notre Dame, August 25, 2002.

[27] Ibid.

[28] Ibid.

[29] Ibid.

determination and creativity. This moves us to the realization that human freedom is not simply tolerated and merely permitted, but is willed as part of an ongoing exchange of divine and human love.[30] Human creativity may thus not be reduced to merely radical subjectivity.[31] We no longer need to be reduced to an obedience that is suspicious of creativity and self-determination, as if the actions of the human person were somehow *ipso facto* divorced from objectivity.[32] At the same time, on the other hand, the truth of the Incarnation does not permit the human person to use his or her self-determination or creativity in the context of a nihilistic self-invention.[33] A notable difference, however, between the human will in Christ and the will of the human person is that while there is not movement in the human will of Christ because it was always in constant union with the divine will, there is always movement proper to the will of the human person, because the freedom always remains to choose not to follow the divine will. Through deliberation and execution of the human will in accord with the eternal *Logos* of Christ, a *hexis*, or according to the Western mind, a *habitus* is formed in the human person that intermingles with the divine.[34] For Maximus, the fire of divine union forged by the hypostatic union pushes human nature

---

[30] Ibid.

[31] Ibid.

[32] Ibid.

[33] Ibid.

[34] P.G. RENCZES, S.J., "Philosophical Anthropology of Saint Maximus the Confessor," 62.

to act in a divine way without violating its own nature.[35] This union of humanity and divinity manifests what Maximus calls a "theandric energy."[36] The rich fruit of this process is that human creativity and the particular moral choices that one makes for the good, in accord with the enteral *Logos*, are granted an eternal and eschatological validity as God receives them.[37] When the human person clearly has this union of will formed in his or her self, his or her will is most effectively an analogy to the union of natures in Christ, and this most effectively disposes the person to the movement from creation to the final end of total and complete divinization. We are thus able to discern in Maximus's rich theological anthropology of the divinization of the human person and the humanization of God, an inchoate sacramentality of human personhood.

## 5.6 The *Logos* and the *Logoi*

The cosmic metaphysic by which the relationship between the Father, the Divine Person of Jesus, and the human person is realized is by way of the distinction between the enteral *Logos* of the second person of the Holy Trinity, Jesus Christ, and the *logoi* of all created being. Through the *Logos* comes to be both being and continuing to be. One finds the cosmological foundations established by Maximus in his *Questiones ad Thallassium* 60 stating: "Because of Christ—or rather, the whole mystery of Christ—all the ages of time and the

---

[35] A. MARCO, "Maximus the Confessor's answer to the crisis of meaning," Church Life Journal.

[36] Ibid.

[37] Ibid.

beings within those ages have received their beginning and end in Christ."[38] Theologian Aidan Nichols, O.P. believes that this is Maximus's most celebrated statement of the hypostatic union as the foundation and goal of the cosmos itself.[39] The *logoi* are understood as the Father's will, actually imprinted within every particular created being. They are a portion of God, yet distinct from God as being created and not eternal. It is only by movement that the *logoi* participate in God. The *logoi* receive their being at creation, and their movement is realized in their attraction to the divine *Logos*. Furthermore, regarding human personhood, the imprint of the *Logos* is tailored toward the particularity of the person, which must give full freedom to the particular choices that the human person will make, and this is properly the foundation for how the Father's will and human freedom interact.[40] As noted above this dynamic interchange will be marked by both radical transcendence, and radical immanence in the constant and perpetual humanization of God and the constant and perpetual divinization of the human person through movement. The dynamic nature of being, movement, is therefore proper to the created order, understood as something positive and in transition toward its cosmic, or eschatological, consummation.

---

[38] See MAXIMUS THE CONFESSOR, *On The Cosmic Mystery of Jesus Christ: Selected Writings from St. Maximus the Confessor*, eds P. M. BLOWERS, R.L. WILKEN St. Vladimir Seminary Press, 2003, 125.

[39] Cf. A. NICHOLS, O.P., "Byzantine Gospel: Maximus the Confessor" in *Modern Scholarship*, Edinburgh, 1993, 135. See A. RIOU, *Le Monde Et L'Église Selon Maxime Le Confesseur*, 95-96.

[40] Ibid.

*Gaudium et Spes* Article 22, widely accepted as the hermeneutical key to the Pastoral Constitution for the life of the Christian in the modern world, reveals the following: "Christ, the final Adam, by the revelation of the mystery of the Father and His love, fully reveals man to himself and makes his supreme calling clear." [41] We see this hermeneutic clearly in Maximus as the Father in the eternal *Logos*, reveals the nature of the *logoi* back to his or her self, as a whole reveals its parts. Maximus in the *Ambigua* 7, makes the distinction between the *Logos* and the *logoi*:

> If by reason and wisdom a person has come to understand that what exists was brought out of non-being into being by God, if he intelligently directs the soul's imagination to the infinite differences and variety of things as they exist by nature and turns his questing eye with understanding towards the intelligible model (logos) according to which things have been made, would he not know that the one Logos is many *logoi*? This is evident in the incomparable differences among created things. For each is unmistakably unique in itself and its identity remains distinct in relation to other things. He will also know that the many *logoi* are the one *Logos* to whom all things are related and who exists in himself without

[41] GAUDIUM ET SPES, *Pastoral Constitution of the Church in the Modern World*, The Second Vatican Council, 1965, Article 22.

confusion, the essential and individually distinctive God, the Logos of God the Father.[42]

All created things are defined in essence by their own *logoi.* Greek Orthodox Professor Reverend Nikolaus Loudovikos states that these *logoi* are understood by Maximus as inherently containing a call and a response dynamic, facilitating a "dialogic reciprocity."[43] In his *Mystagogia* Maximus states that all beings are led in a "common and unconfused identity of movement and existence" back toward their origin, the Father.[44] In this light, the motion or movement that is proper to created being for Maximus is inclusive of dialogue.[45]

In fact, the call to dialogue is imprinted in the very nature of each *logoi.* Christ, the *Logos,* actually speaks personally to, and remains personally present to, each *logoi* and calls each person by name. There is a "spiritual DNA" inscribed in the *logoi* that may be described as a particular "blueprint" for the person with which to cooperate. The dialogue of the human person and the *Logos* occurs

---

[42] MAXIMUS THE CONFESSOR, *Ambigua* 7, in *On The Cosmic Mystery of Jesus Christ: Selected Writings from St. Maximus the Confessor*, eds., P. M. Blowers, R.L. Wilken, 54-55.

[43] N. LOUDOVIKOS, *Eucharistic Ontology: Maximus the Confessor's Eschatological Ontology of Being as Dialogical Reciprocity*, Holy Cross Orthodox Press, Brookline, MA, 2010, 201-206. See also A. MARCO, "Maximus the Confessor's answer to the crisis of meaning," Church Life Journal.

[44] MAXIMUS THE CONFESSOR, *Mystagogia* 1, in *The Classics of Western Spirituality*, ed., J. Farina, 186.

[45] A. MARCO, "Maximus the Confessor's answer to the crisis of meaning," Church Life Journal.

throughout a lifetime and is realized through one's choosing moral actions in accord with what comes to be known through the dialogue. Therefore, the concept of the *logoi* cuts through the thicket of the perceived dichotomy of obedience and the self-invention that is both inherent and necessary for the fullness of personal freedom to be realized.[46] The *logoi* are "individuated expressions" that anchor all created things in God and set them on their path for their eschatological return to the Father.[47] Furthermore, this return occurs through the dialogical exchange between the *logoi* and the one *Logos* which gives order and universal purpose to all of creation. Maximus thus provides a metaphysic for explaining that God's intention for persons not only extends to human nature as a whole, but also to the intended particular nature of each person in his or her created uniqueness.[48]

When each *logoi* responds to the *Logos*, he or she is acting according to his or her human nature, and according to the nature of the Father expressed through His will, which is expressed in the love of the Son to all creation. While each individual and created soul does not pre-exist in the eternal Son, the Father nevertheless indeed has known loved and willed the creation of each human person eternally before the actual human person was created. Every person is eternally conceived in the love of the Father in his eternal Son, and is therefore called to return to his eternal embrace in this great Christological dynamic of *exitus* and *reditus*. Creation, inclusive of

[46] Ibid.
[47] Ibid.
[48] Ibid.

the human person, is always proper and ontologically other, and the response to each created person to the will of the Father is realized through responding to the call extended by name through the *Logos* of the Son, and the response is thus most properly and metaphysically understood in the form of a response to a call.[49] The *Logos* provides the order, meaning and direction for all of creation.[50]

The *Logos* is actually the natural will within the human person, which is in perfect accord with the eternal *Logos*. The human person, therefore, must thus freely choose to remain in the *Logos*, the natural will, perfected in the person of Christ, and act according to the plan of the *Logos* for the *logoi* to possess true ontological value, or else risk the loss of the ontological value by falling into the non-being of sin, and lose his or her unique otherness altogether.[51] Choosing outside of the love of the Father would violate the ontology of his or her existence itself and thus result in nothingness. The path of our ontology has been pre-set by the Father within the eternal *Logos*, Jesus, before our creation, all with leaving our human freedom completely integral through the presence of the *Logos*, or the inherent capacity within each person to will in accord with God's particular plan for each of us.

---

[49] Ibid.

[50] Ibid.

[51] Ibid.

## 5.7 Tropos

The Father had an idea of his particular plan for each of us, and for our distinct purpose in his eternal mind, and this is expressed in the *logoi*. Maximus states that each of the *logoi* are equipped with a gnomic will, which possesses the faculty to deliberate and choose. The *tropos* is understood by Maximus to be the manner, or the way by which the person chooses to exercise his or her will. For Maximus, the deliberation, and choice, of the acts for the good are accomplished by the *gnome*, or gnomic will of the human person. The gnomic will signifies a permanent potential to pass from a fundamental position to another position in the engagement of the will in relation to the *Logos*. It is therefore clearly a personal disposition tending toward a finality. The gnomic will is conditioned by the choices and events that are unique and particular to the life of each person, thus marking upon those circumstances the eternal mark of not only the subjective, but also the eternally eschatological. This will pertains to the mystery of each human being as a *logoi*, and thus makes the *logoi* deeply personal. The gnomic will has the freedom to choose in accord with the *Logos*, or towards non-being, or evil, which is outside of the *Logos*, who always contains the perfect orientation of the human will, as it did in Jesus.

Further to the anthropological contribution, for Maximus the *hexis* is the *Logos* within the human person. The *hexis*, as the *Logos*, is something greater than the moral choice which the human person makes, and the manner or mode in which he or she makes it, but it at the same time fully includes this subjective component. It is a stabilizing presence within the human person that is formed by virtue of the choices that the human person makes in communion with the *Logos* within him or her. Insofar as it functions in this regard it is likened to the concept of *habitus* in Saint Thomas.

The concept of *hexis* is found in both Plato and Aristotle. For Plato, the concept is understood as the disposition of the soul for the good, or as a comportment for a specific occupation. For Aristotle, the concept of *hexis* is found in his *Nicomachean Ethics*. For Plato and Aristotle it corresponds to the nature within the human person, a state, that corresponds to the good, a deeply ingrained quality of character that disposes one to act in a certain way. Furthermore, Maximus states that while Christ possessed a natural will in his integral humanity, a gnomic will is only proper to the human person in the fallen state. The gnomic will, the *hexis* and the *Logos* are therefore all present within the human person, the *logoi*. The *hexis* forms the gnomic will, and as the gnomic will makes choices in accord with the *Logos* by the exercise of the gnomic will, the *hexis* has more an effect on the gnomic will as the *hexis* becomes a stronger and more stabilizing presence within the *logoi*, thus orienting through the practice of virtue, the human person to choose in accord with the *Logos*.

The subjective becomes even more developed in Maximus through the *tropos*, which illustrates the mode or the manner in which the gnomic will is exercised, thus also contributing to this highly subjective component of the practice of virtue to the ontological. For example, an illustrative example of the distinct particularity of this synergistic and dynamic process would be in acquiring the mastery of playing a musical instrument. The virtue to play a musical instrument through the practice of a performing art, through choice, and in accord with the spiritual imprint of our *logoi,* through *tropos* becomes part of our being. One first makes the particular choice of the instrument (string, brass, woodwind, percussion). *Tropos* becomes even more particular, as the way, manner or mode in which the instrument is played (Classical, Jazz, Folk, Contemporary). Such particular details actually become embedded in being and ontological and enduring eschatologically and particularly through their participation in the *Logos.* Thus, when this unique mode or manner in which a virtue is exercised becomes part of our being it is no longer merely subjective or accidental, but "ontologically subjective," as it is now united with the *Logos* and thus, eschatological and eternal. Not only is the playing of the musical instrument in a particular manner now part of the being of the person as united with the eternal *Logos*, but the choice of the style of music is also part of the being of the person as well.

The *Opuscula* 1 confirms that Maximus uses the metaphysical distinctions of the Cappadocian Fathers for wider use[52] by the use of the term *tropos,* which is fundamentally a Trinitarian distinction first found in the Cappadocian Fathers, but is nevertheless also

---

[52] See P.G. Renczes, *Agir De Dieu et Liberté de L'Homme*, 25, to understand the influence of the Cappadocian Fathers, as well as Pseudo-Dionysius the Areopagite, on Maximus the Confessor. In the thought of Gregory of Nyssa (335-394), Cappadocian Father, we find *kinesis*, movement, as the human will is prominent in his thought, and the human will is always in movement in the choice for good or evil.

applied to human existence by Maximus.[53] As noted above, the *tropos* is the manner, or mode, in which the human person lives and makes moral choices, a significant existential contribution pertaining to the ontology of personhood. Contributing further to its existential application to the human person,[54] Maximus states in *Ambigua* 42 the following:

> Generally speaking, all innovation is manifested in relation to the mode (*tropos*) of the thing innovated, not its natural principle (*logos*). The principle, if it undergoes innovation, corrupts the nature, as the nature in that case does not maintain inviolate the principle according to which it exists. The mode thus innovated, while the natural principle is preserved, displays a miraculous power, insofar as the nature appears to be acted upon, and to act, clearly beyond its normal scope.[55]

When the *tropos* aligns with the *Logos* in the created person of the *logoi*, the person experiences particular growth and well-being, and is illumined and empowered through innovation and creativity.

---

[53] See A. RIOU, *Le Monde Et L'Église Selon Maxime Le Confesseur*, 39 for a historical account of how Maximus would have been in contact with the whole of the Cappadocian tradition.

[54] A. LOUTH, *Selected Essays, Volume 1: Studies in Patristics*, Chapter 28, L. AYRES, and J. BEHR (eds), Oxford University Press, 2023, 305-311.

[55] MAXIMUS THE CONFESSOR, *Ambigua* 42, in *On The Cosmic Mystery of Jesus Christ: Selected Writings from St. Maximus the Confessor*, eds., P. M. Blowers and R.L. Wilken, 90.

The creativity is reflected in the way the person is uniquely called to act, pertaining to the *tropos*. In the return of the *logoi* to God, this particular mode or manner of acting, now marked ontologically due to the graces of the hypostatic union, and the participation of humanity in divinity within this cosmic metaphysic, truly ontologically stamps and gathers all that has been truly and uniquely that of the *logoi* during his or her earthly pilgrimage. As *tropos* is the existential way the *logoi* live out their particular mission, every particular unique detail of our lives are both informed by the eschatological, and contribute to the unique share and participation in the person as eschatological.

The metaphysical reality of what we are choosing to identify for the purpose of this project as "ontological subjectivity" opens up new horizons for metaphysics as it metaphysically incorporates the unique and particular dimension of personhood into our understanding of being, making these characteristics and qualities, often affective in their nature, as part of being and personhood that at the same time is hoped to lead to an understanding of personhood as sacramental. Personhood is sacramental because it is at the same time both ontologically connected with the divine and so deeply particular that one person can be said to contain the whole in a manner that passing one over would be to miss gazing upon a whole part of the splendor of creation, in a manner similar to choosing not to look up at the beauty of a mountain when passing through a National Park. Furthermore, the absence of one is therefore felt as the absence of the whole, in the same manner as if one chooses to not look up at the beauty of a mountain, something would be missing from his or her trip.

Another illustrative example would be in the creative pursuit of a visual art. The potential to become a good painter, sculpture, architect, or poet may be imprinted in our *logoi*, but becoming a good artist, for example, is only fulfilled in the free and deliberate choices that the person makes to devote his or her self to the concentrated practice of painting so as to acquire knowledge and skill. The practice and discipline of the virtue of painting leads to a uniquely practicing diligent artist painting in the manner that the Father has designed for the person, created through the *Logos* as *logoi* has uniquely designed for him or her.

The same may said about study as every human person has the capacity to become learned and wise, however we only become learned and wise by deliberate acts of the will that choose learning and wisdom within the dynamic movement of the person through life and in accord with the field of study or particular trade that is imprinted within our *logoi* to practice. With the practice of study in a field of research (Humanities, Environmental Science, Economics, or Medicine) or learning and practice in a Skilled Trade (Plumber, Bricklayer, Boilermaker, Electrician, Welder, Carpenter) the unique manner or mode in which one cooperates with the "spiritual DNA" imprinted within his or her *logoi* contributes to the dynamic expansion and growth of their humanity in the *Logos* in the particular field in accord with the *Logos*, thus contributing to the overall synergy of the human and divine cooperation in the cosmic liturgy, realized as a whole in the unique and particular reality of each created person.

Playing a musical instrument, becoming a good artist, becoming learned and wise, and mastering a trade all become part of the being of the person through the *hexis*, and by virtue of this concept, distinct moral qualities are no longer accidental, but are brought up into the divine life through the hypostatic union, by way of analogy through the endless exchange of loving communion. Within this whole dynamic, and in analogical accord with the distinct and unseparated, unconfused and unmixed relationship between the two natures in the Christ as defined at the Fourth Ecumenical Council of Chalcedon (451), the human operations are neither assimilated with the divine, nor separated from the divine.

Freedom is therefore something more than obeying the Father's will in a strict manner, something beyond the minimal acceptance or rejection of the Father's will. Rather, freedom is so deeply personal and dynamic that one could never understand it as uniform or monolithic. While each *logoi* is obliged by the order of creation to be faithful to this ontology so that he or she may love truly according to the purpose of their nature, so as to be free of all natural and unruly passions, each person will exercise this freedom in the most ample and infinite space that is given to him or her according to the total integrity of the human will of the person. This thus offers more appreciation for the full ontology of what it means to be a person, and the great gift that this sacramentality is to others, as others are drawn and attracted to affective uniqueness of the other as they enter into dialogue and communion with others.

Essentially, if human freedom is a willed part of the ongoing exchange of love in this metaphysical dynamic, then the choices that constitute the orientation of personhood may by no means be regarded as somehow non-essential to the being of the person as related to the Holy Trinity. The hypostatic union, on the other hand, calls for an endless exchange of loving communion in the context of the lived reality of daily existence, as Maximus helps us realize how by analogy the union of the divine and human in Jesus is extended to the Christian by grace. Anthony Marco describes this as having a "tropic impact.[56]"

The Father's will for humanity, in this perspective, may be metaphysically understood in the form of a dialogue with the human person which contains an infinite number of possibilities according to each particular *logoi.*[57] Dialogue itself becomes a dynamic manifestation of being and growth in virtue, and it requires otherness, both on a human and divine level. Marco observes that according to Maximus, when we return to the Father in our humanity, we will be "clothed with the particularity of our decisions and creativity."[58]

## 5.8 The Ongoing Search for Personhood

We have thus observed that, well before the advent of modernity in the late 19th century, which was marked by the search for "ontological subjectivity," the seventh century Maximus the Confessor was providing an appropriately existential response to these necessary questions. It would therefore be rather uncritical, and a grave pastoral omission, to dismiss modern questions by not addressing them with appropriately existential responses founded in truth. One must dive deeper into the history of theology to find more adequate responses, surprisingly more conducive to adequate pastoral responses to longings, than some forms of medieval scholasticism were able to provide due to historical circumstances.

---

[56] A. MARCO, "Maximus the Confessor's answer to the crisis of meaning," Church Life Journal.

[57] Ibid.

[58] Ibid.

The Maximian contribution is that the subjective participation in the objective renders the subjective a participation in the personhood of the eternal. This participation could thus be described as the human person being a sign and instrument of the eternal *Logos* in the sense that the subjective elements of the human person (his or her identity and decisions) are used by God in such a way as to make evident an eschatological ontology. Thus, since the human person, in his or her participation in the *Logos* as a *logoi*, is a kind of sacrament of personhood.

Nevertheless, while it is evident that Maximus is an Eastern Patristic source for a much needed human phenomenological light upon Trinitarian ontological distinctions,[59] which more effectively provide answers to these modern questions, despite his metaphysical depth, we at the same time do not find in him the final linguistic answers to describe the indescribable, which is the sacramentality of personhood for which we seek. We therefore must continue our search both philosophically and theologically, having settled upon this metaphysical foundation. Within the security of a Trinitarian metaphysic which Maximus has provided us, we now turn to a Trinitarian informed ecclesiology that properly responds to these anthropological questions, as we continue to remain open to the contribution of philosophy to take us on an even greater journey into the depth of the mystery for which we long, the sacramentality of personhood.

---

[59] H. U. BALTHASAR, *Cosmic Liturgy*, 63.

# Chapter Six

# Metropolitan John Zizioulas: Person as Beyond Substance

"He is before all things, and in him all things hold together" (Col 1:17)

## 6.1 Western Limitations

*Persona est naturae rationalis individua substantia* (A Person is an individual substance of a rational nature). This was the definition of the person established by the Roman Senator, historian and philosopher of the Early Middle Ages Boethius (ca. 480-524). He was a precursor of the Scholastic movement and a leading Christian scholar of the 6th century. His definition for human personhood marked a foundational definition for subsequent Western thought. The problem with this definition is that it lacks a proper Trinitarian reference by analogy and identifies the human person as definable within his or her self, thus isolating the human person as an individual. As David Walsh understands persons to be analogues of God and that God is the source of their analogical reality, we are truly able to see how far this Boethian definition of the sixth century is from the developed understanding of person as we have discovered with Walsh in the twenty-first century. The difference not only has intellectual consequences, but spiritual and pastoral consequences as well.

## 6.2 Pastoral Illustration – Love and Personhood found in Pets

An experienced Pastor of many years recently recalled to us how he chose to address the question of children wondering the eternal destination of their dog after death. The Pastor, choosing a purely substance based approach to a sensitive pastoral question, responded by stating that only the "doginess" of the dog goes to heaven, thus stressing the substance of the dog over the totality of the dog, for the reason of the dog being substantially irrational, and thus not a person. While metaphysically faithful to Western metaphysics, the answer is pastorally unfeasible and unnecessarily restricted. While a dog is philosophically irrational, the reason why they are so lovable, and why children are concerned about their eternal destination, is because they mirror personhood. The child thus sees characteristics of personhood in the dog that the child loves. Personhood again here takes primacy over substance, insofar as a substance based answer could actually be more harmful than beneficial to the emotional and spiritual well-being of the child presenting the question. The Pastor, Scholastically well-trained in philosophy, nevertheless lacked the proper philosophical understanding of the value of love and personhood with regards to being. It would have been more pastorally feasible for the Pastor to affirm that the child found characteristics of love in the dog, and that love comes from God, and God brings all things to himself that he has created out of love, without mentioning the unnecessary substantial "doginess" in his response to the question. Essentially, the child's question was not about the substance of the dog, but about the characteristics of love and personhood that were experienced in the presence of the dog. In this case, therefore, addressing substance alone completely derailed the child's question from finding its proper end, which was a movement from an experience of the characteristics of love and personhood to truth.

## 6.3 Contemporary Greek Eastern Openings

Greek Orthodox Metropolitan John Zizioulas studied first at the University of Athens and University of Thessaloniki, and then under Russian Orthodox theologian Georges Florovsky (1893-1979) of the Russian Orthodox Church at Harvard University, taught at the University of Edinburgh, and Glasgow, was the Chair of the Academy of Athens, and was a leading theological contributor to the Ecumenical dialogue between the East and the West. His distinguished theological career, deeply immersed in Patristic metaphysics, highlighted this significant metaphysical problem throughout his comprehensive ecumenical theological project, which helped bridge the divide between the East and the West, as he advocated a more patristic theological hermeneutic of personhood and communion, which established him as one of the most influential Orthodox Christian theologians of the 20th and 21st centuries. Metropolitan Zizioulas died in 2023 and is buried at the First Cemetery of Athens. He told his doctoral students, with whom he would often gather and share fellowship and theological conversation, that he always found God in the horizontal form of human relationships more than the vertical dimension of the unseen. Yet, it was in the sacred space of these horizontal relationships that led him deeply into the ontology of liturgical worship as the fundamental understanding of all existence.

## 6.4 Ratzinger; Richard of Saint Victor; and Saint Thomas Aquinas

The approach to personhood found in the Scottish theologian and philosopher Richard of St. Victor (+1173) in his 12th century, *Treatise on the Trinity*, exemplifies the need to go beyond the philosophical definition of person as found in Boethius. In Richard of St. Victor, the divine person is understood as *ex-sistentia*. Balthasar understands the existential ramifications of this definition, commenting that "person is regarded as a spiritual subject that earns the name *person* only by going out beyond itself (ex)-in God as something relative."[1] Thomas Aquinas also seems to appreciate the insufficiency of Boethius' definition when it pertains to defining divine personhood.[2] Aquinas therefore turns to Richard for a more adequate definition, citing Richard's definition of person: "Person in God is the incommunicable existence of the divine nature."[3] Articulating the

---

[1] H.U. Balthasar, *On the Concept of Person*, Communio, (US), V.13, Spring 1986, 18-26.

[2] See Thomas Aquinas, *Summa Theologiae* 1, q.29 a.3, Reply Obj. 2. Thomas attempts to relate the Boethian definition of person to divine personhood by the understanding of "dignity". "Because subsistence in a rational nature is of high dignity, therefore every individual of rational nature is called a 'person'. Now the dignity of the divine nature excels every other dignity; and thus the name person pre-eminently belongs to God".

[3] Thomas Aquinas, *Summa Theologiae* 1, q.29 a.3, Reply Obj. 4.

relationship between this definition and human personhood, Aquinas states: "The word person is not used in an equivocal sense. Though neither is it applied univocally, since nothing can be said univocally of God and creatures."[4] While the relationship between divine and human personhood is implied, it was not developed in Thomas' work, yet at the same time we see Saint Thomas searching for similarities between Divine and human personhood, despite the limitations inherent in his search. Regarding the concept of 'person', Saint Thomas states: "Although this name person may not belong to God as regards the origin of the term, nevertheless it objectively belongs to God in its objective meaning"[5].

Later, Joseph Ratzinger manifests the weakness of Richard's definition and that of Thomas Aquinas. He asserts that at the beginning of the Middle Ages theologians did not apply categories to the whole extent of spiritual reality but limited them to Christ and the Trinity.[6] Failing to integrate an understanding of person illumined by the Trinity means that person is defined solely as the rational individual or according to psychological experience, thus left inadequately treated. Zizioulas describes the tragic results:

> With the help of a cross-fertilization between the Boethian and the Augustinian approaches to man, our Western philosophy and culture have formed a concept of man out of combination of two basic components: *rational individuality*

[4] THOMAS AQUINAS, *Summa Theologiae* 1, q.29 a.4, Reply Obj. 4.

[5] THOMAS AQUINAS, *Summa Theologiae* 1, q.29 a.3, Reply Obj. 2.

[6] Cf. J. RATZINGER, *Retrieving the Tradition: Concerning the notion of person in theology*, Communio (US), V.17, (Fall 1990), 440-454.

on the one hand and psychological experience and consciousness on the other. It was on the basis of this combination that Western thought arrived at the conception of the person as an *individual* and/or *personality*, that is, a unit endowed with intellectual, psychological and moral qualities centered on the axis of consciousness. Man's distinctive characteristic became in this way identical with his ability to be conscious of himself and of others and thus to be an autonomous self who intends, thinks, decides, acts, and produces results.[7]

## 6.5 Western Limitations Remain

The Western philosophical understanding of person has become the modern understanding of person. The American J.R. Meyer defines our modern understanding thus: "A conscious, rational individual, an autonomous self, who thinks, intends, chooses, act, and produces various results."[8] According to Meyer, these qualities are not sufficient, for they do not adequately distinguish human beings from other sentient creatures.[9] Meyer turns to Zizioulas for another definition of the human person, for a definition that understands

---

[7] J.D. Zizioulas, *Communion and Otherness*, T & T Clarke, 2006, 210-211.

[8] J.R. Meyer, *An Ek-static View of the Person*, Josephinum Journal of Theology, Vol.8, Winter/Spring 2001, 12.

[9] Cf. J.R. Meyer, *An Ek-static View of the Person*, 122. Here Meyer makes reference to the growing scientific opinion that reason and communication do not separate man from the other animals.

personhood as distinct from being an individual, where personhood is understood to transcend the boundaries of the self[10] and thus provides true freedom. Personhood must include the capability to break through boundaries in search of communion.[11]

## 6.6 THE NEED FOR THE EAST: PERSON DEFINED BY RELATION

In contrast to this Western understanding of person, Zizioulas conceives of the person in terms of relation. He states that being a person is basically different than being an individual or 'personality' in that the person cannot be conceived in itself as a static entity, but only as it relates to another."[12]A person must go out of his or self to discover self. Notably, the position of Zizioulas compares both with Hans Urs von Balthasar and Joseph Ratzinger in the West, who both criticize the Boethian definition. Balthasar questions how an individual of itself can describe a spiritual nature.[13] Joseph Ratzinger states that the Boethian definition of person which prevails in Western philosophy is entirely insufficient.[14] Ratzinger, like Zizioulas,

---

[10] Cf. J.D. ZIZIOULAS *Human Capacity and Incapacity*: *A Theological Exploration of Personhood, Scottish Journal of Theology*, V. 28, (1975) as found in Communion and Otherness, 210-212.

[11] Cf. J.R. MEYER, *An Ek-static View of the Person*, 122.

[12] J.D. ZIZIOULAS, *Communion and Otherness*, 210-213.

[13] See H.U. BALTHASAR, *On the Concept of Person*, Communio (US) Vol. 13, (Spring) 1986, 18-26.

[14] Cf. J. RATZINGER,, *Retrieving the Tradition: Concerning the notion of person in theology*, 448.

prefers to understand personhood theologically, not in substantialist but more in existential terms.[15]

Notwithstanding the centuries of value that the use of the Greek term *ousia*, substance, has contributed to theology, most notably to Trinitarian theology, there have nevertheless been some significant limitations to the use of term with regards to the philosophical development of the notion of personhood in relation to Trinitarian theology, and in particular in relationship to the substantial divinity of Christ, and the insertion of the human person within the grace of the divinity of the Son of God by virtue of his human nature. The problem of individualism has become such a widespread social problem that a more adequate theological and philosophical response is certainly demanded. The human person is constituted politically and does not flourish apart from other human persons within the lived reality of politics.[16] In fact, it is apparent to all responsible persons of good will that the highest rational, logical, or natural experience of fulfillment in humanity is within the context of a community, where reciprocal love is shared among persons. Essentially, this experience of communion within natural fellowship, or politics, becomes the highest philosophical proof for a Trinitarian God, and manifests a deep thirst for a theology of persons to more deeply illumine this experience from the perspective of ontology.

Furthermore, the problem of individualism, increased dramatically in recent times within our post-Christian and secularized

---

[15] Ibid.

[16] See ARISTOTLE, *Politics*, Loeb Classical Library, Harvard University Press, 1932.

world, marked by the tyranny of technology and Social Media and the rise of an abuse of the good of Artificial Intelligence, gives rise to some rather necessary and deep ontological questions which begin with the nature of the thing, and the ontology of the person in his or her self. Zizioulas's life-long project was to address the problem of the dissociation of the created being, inclusive of the human person, to ontological communion with God.

## 6.7 A New Life as a Gateway for Ontology

Respect for man's 'personal identity' is perhaps the most fundamental desire of the human person.[17] Substance alone cannot quench this existential thirst. This is what first attracted us to the theology of Zizioulas, as he understood well this fundamental question posed by the human person, and he provided a deeply ecclesial and theological response. Yet at the same time, he reverses the existentialist conception of particularity by emphasizing that we do not create our own particularity and uniqueness in person-hood, but that this uniqueness is given to us only by ontology.[18] Both the desire for communion and fellowship with other persons, and the retention of particularity within that experience of communion, are the highest of the natural desires of the human person. Intrinsic to the desire for personal identity is the search for freedom, itself a fundamental desire of mankind. Human persons notably seek this freedom of personal identity by identifying with something that is

---

[17] J.D. Zizioulas, *Being As Communion*, 27.

[18] J.D. ZIZOULAS, *Communion and Otherness*, 215-216.

common to a fellowship of persons where communion is experienced, yet the personal identity is maintained and even enhanced by the affirmation of the other. Persons are often looking to go outside of themselves to discover themselves. Yet, with these natural group identifications, while often very good in themselves, such groups do not evade the ontological tragedy of the death of the persons with whom they are experiencing fellowship and communion.[19] Substance cannot offer the longing for affirmation, trust, acceptance and the affective awareness that only personhood can provide. Personhood moves beyond the logical and analytical analysis of a situation and carries the uniqueness and particular discernment with respect for the persons, personalities and temperaments that every conflict involving persons requires. For the fulfillment of personhood, and to evade the question of death, persons will need an ontology and eschatology that Zizioulas describes is found primarily in the communion of the Holy Eucharist, which we will explain in greater detail in Chapter Eight.

---

[19] See J.D. ZIZIOULAS, *Communion and Otherness*, 214. Here Zizioulas, in using the thought of Dostoevsky, speaks of personhood as either leading to God, or to non-existence. See C. P. SCHROEDER, "Suffering Toward Personhood: John Zizioulas and Fyodor Dostoevsky" *In Conversation On Freedom and the Human Person*, St. Vladimir Theological Quarterly, V. 45, 2001, 243-264. Schroeder compares the similarities here between these two Eastern thinkers and compares their analysis of the limitations of the created order, and the inevitability of suffering as a created being.

## 6.8 Christ Overcomes the Natural Tragedy of Death

For Zizioulas, division is essential to the relationship between God and creation, but it is overcome through Christ's restoration of the cosmos. The spatial-temporal dimension of the created order is essentially different from God and thus different from the person of Christ. Therefore, the human person, a priest of creation according to Maximus the Confessor, becomes the bridge of communion between the created and the uncreated in Christ.[20] For Zizioulas, the inherent problem of creation is death, for death reveals that nature is not the ultimate answer to communion, and something beyond nature, such as the Holy Eucharist, is essential. Death exists because communion and otherness cannot coincide in creation.[21] Likewise, the Fall ultimately reveals the tragic dangers that are inherent to

---

[20] See N.V. Harrison, *Zizioulas on Communion and Otherness*, St. Vladimir Theological Quarterly, V. 42, 1998, 273-300. Harrison argues that the position of Zizioulas regarding the person is the bridge between the created and the uncreated is a distinction which is at odds with the patristic teaching on the divine energies, which provides a manner of explaining that God is fully present in creation, while still remain distinct from his essence. While Zizioulas, on the other hand, makes creation dependent upon the person for participation in God. See A. Papanikolaou, *Divine Energies or Divine Personhood: Vladimir Lossky and John Zizioulas on Conceiving the Transcendent and Immanent God*, Modern Theology, V. 19, July 2003, 358-383. Here the distinction is made between the difference between the use of energies by Russian Orthodox theologian Vladmir Lossky (1903-1958) for the distinction between the created and the uncreated, and the use of personhood by Zizioulas.

[21] J.D. Zizioulas, *Communion and Otherness*, 216-217.

creation if it is left to itself. Ultimately, because of the Fall, the problem between communion and otherness that is inherent to creation is exacerbated by individualization. The Fall reveals the tragedy, according to Zizioulas, of the failure to make being dependent upon communion.[22]

## 6.9 Freedom beyond Individualization yet in Difference

Difference, and therefore otherness, is proper to creation by virtue of its spatial-temporal character and must not be turned into division by the tragedy of individualization. According to Zizioulas, the dying being is a contradiction in the most absurd terms.[23] For Zizioulas, the dying being is philosophical proof that truth cannot be coextensive with nature, and thus something more than substance is needed to define personhood. It is on this premise that Zizioulas rejects the identification of truth with nature, and fundamentally calls for a renewed metaphysics based in personhood. The dying being falsifies truth at the level of nature.[24] Despite the existential fear of death, the human person does not respond to it ontologically; rather he or she self-identifies through the qualities of nature and seeks protection based on those qualities, despite the reality of natural death that awaits them.[25] Tragedy results because

---

[22] Cf. J.D. Zizioulas, *Being As Communion,* 102.

[23] Ibid., 105.

[24] Ibid., 105.

[25] Cf. J.D. Zizioulas, *Communion and Otherness*, 217-218. Person implies not simply the freedom to have different qualities, but mainly the

difference is continually turned into division. Ultimately, because of a lack of ontology, different beings become distant beings: because difference becomes division, distinction becomes distance.[26] Humanity turns difference into division through rejection of the other. The tragedy that difference becomes division is ultimately the tragedy of the fear of the other and, above all, fear of all otherness.[27]

For Zizioulas, natural being is falsified by the natural death, and thus an ontological approach to personhood is the only possible response to death and the tragic limitations of the natural order.[28] Only personhood gives a true ontological understanding of personal identity. Therefore, he responds to the questions from the post-modern or the post-Christian person[29] with an ecclesial Anthro-

---

freedom to simply be yourself. Freedom is only understood in Zizioulas, however, in the absolute ontological sense.

[26] Ibid., 219.

[27] Ibid., 227.

[28] Ibid., 228.

[29] See D.A. FISHER, *Byzantine Ontology: Reflections on the thought of John Zizioulas*, in Diakonia, Vol. 29, 1996, 58. Here Fisher describes our era as an era that may be labeled as post-modern, contemporary, or even post-Christian. He states that it is an era concerned above all things with personal identity. See W. KASPER, *Church as Communio*, Communio (US), Vol. 13,1986, 100. Over forty years ago, Kasper provided a very accurate assessment of the technological trends that bring people together outwardly while, however, there remains within this trend only separated individuals who remain isolated and lonely. Kasper accurately notes that modern technological collectivism is not a proper response to the problem of individualism. In a collectively technological world people will continue to rely upon their own nature for differentiation, only to find they remain in a state of isolation and loneliness. The person in the communion of the Church, he argues, gives the person happiness and peace only in personal

pology. Zizioulas concludes that the post-modern understanding of identity did not involve an ontological understanding of particularity. Rather, it is a perceived desire for freedom based on *differentiation* from the other.[30] Understanding this deep desire for differentiation, we were drawn to Zizioulas in our first project because he offers an eschatological and ecclesial identity, inviting the person to truly discover themselves in a category beyond nature, overcoming the limitations of nature, and thus offering an ecclesial response to the desire for differentiation, offering a true ontological particularity.[31] Otherness, a desire of the person for particularity, is often understood only in terms of desiring to be liberated from control and to not be absorbed into a unity wherein diversity is not appreciated. This, in our opinion, is a just reaction to the ideology of modernism.[32] In a 1996 article entitled "Truth and Freedom," Joseph Ratzinger manifests his shared concerns, similar to Zizioulas, in this regard, as he directly engages the problem by stating that the contemporary person extols freedom and places it at the pinnacle of our scale of values.[33]

---

union, in common values and goals, in mutual giving and sharing of personal values.

[30] Cf. J.D. ZIZIOULAS, *Communion and Otherness*, 229.

[31] Ibid., 238.

[32] Ibid., 233

[33] J. RATZINGER, *Truth and Freedom*, Communio US Vol. 23, Spring 1996, 16-35. Here Ratzinger notes the modern man's understanding of freedom is dangerously close to the dream of Karl Marx regarding the future of the communist society, quoting Marx: "to do one thing today and another tomorrow; to hunt in the morning and fish in the afternoon, breed cattle in the evening, and criticize after dinner, just as I please".

## 6.10 Beyond Zizioulas: Ethics; Ontology; Ethics

Zizioulas providentially, in his *corpus* of theological work, begins with the practical and the ethical insofar as his point of departure for communion with the Holy Trinity is the Holy Eucharist. As a consequence, he overlooks how important ethics truly is both in both our discovery of ontology in the Holy Eucharist, and in the moral imperative to live a particular ethic within the *Logos*, after that ontology is discovered. We found, however, even within the work of our first project, that there were limitations to Zizioulas's theology, insofar as his work did not treat adequately the interiority, consciousness, and moral discernment of the person, as his summary dismissal of the Augustinian and Thomistic traditions did not leave space for these necessary ethical contributions of the West for moral theology. Furthermore, at the time of our first and second projects, due to Zizioulas's significant influence, we embraced the language of rights as being problematic, but now almost two decades later we have found that rights language embraces the ethical dimension which Zizioulas overlooked for ontology. After years of reflection, our developed position, following Emmanuel Levinas, is that ethics must precede ontology, and that ethics must be developed after ontology is established. Providentially, we at the same time have found such deep convergence between the thought of Levinas and Zizioulas, as both the philosopher and the theologian understand relationship with others as fundamental to one's identity. The ethical is discovered in the natural, in the human experience of relationality and politics, and that must lead to a Christian ontology, or else it becomes subject to ideology. As Zizioulas's search was a search for personhood, so was the intention of our first and second projects. Neither we nor Zizioulas arrived at a precise answer, but we both participated in the inexorable search for personhood, that alludes nature and must be illumined by theology. It is a philosophical search, but a philosophical search that demands ultimate subjection to theology in its undefinable mystery. We appreciate that it is indeed confounding, for if truth is connected with life, it must begin with ethics, but there is no ontology in ethics, and certainly there is no salvation in ethics. Ethics precedes ontology, but in a fallen world, shackled with the problem of individualism, knowledge sadly takes priority over love.

## 6.11 Art: Presence in Absence

Proper to the spatio-temporal dimension of the created order is the reality that personal identity does not only exist according to the category of substance, observes Zizioulas. Within the created order, a paradox, a mystery, points to personhood as the means of understanding communion and otherness. Zizioulas maintains that presence is achieved in absence within the created order, but only through the understanding of person. In a similar manner to Professor Walsh, Zizioulas uses the example of the creative capacity of art. In order for the artist to establish his or her unique and personal presence in the piece of created art, they must use pre-existing matter, so that they leave something of themselves in what they create, even though they are absent from the work.[34] Thus the artist exists

[34] Cf. J.D. Zizioulas, *Communion and Otherness,* 217.

for the viewer by virtue of absence. Zizioulas describes presence-in-absence as coming from outside the world, a bridge to understanding personhood in God without the danger of anthropomorphism.[35] There is something more mysterious or transcendental about personhood than createdness, something that exceeds the category of substance.

The paradox of presence-in-absence verifies that personal presence cannot be extrapolated from created existence.[36] For Zizioulas, this reality becomes the sign *par excellence* of the creaturely limitation of humanity.[37] It therefore verifies that categories of nature cannot adequately describe personhood. On the contrary, precisely because of this paradox, something that transcends nature is needed. Thus it follows that the substantial quality of a creature does not precede its mode of existence.[38] On the contrary, personhood must be primary and constitutive of substance in order to properly address the objective reality of the mystery insofar as the limitations of nature describe the mystery.[39] Another illustration offered by Zizioulas, based on an example offered by Sartre, is helpful:

> I have an appointment in a café with a friend whose existence matters to me, and on my arrival there I discover that this

---

[35] Ibid., 228.

[36] Ibid., 219. See also R. SOKOLOWSKI, *Presence and Absence,: A Philosophical Investigation of Language and Being,* Bloomington, IN, 1978, 28-29.

[37] Ibid., 226.

[38] Cf. J.R. MEYER, *An Ek-static View of the Person*, 122.

[39] Ibid., 122.

> person is not there, the absent person *precisely by not being there* occupies for me the entire space-time context of the café. It is only *after* I reflect consciously on the situation that I realize empirically who 'is' and who 'is not' there. But as I do that a significant distinction emerges between the presence of personal and the presence of a-personal beings.[40]

Distinguishing the mystery of personhood as a different category from the individual, Zizioulas states: "Personhood prefers to create its presence as absence rather than be contained, comprehended, described, and manipulated through the circumscribability and individualization which are inherent in all creaturehood."[41] Such creation of presence is accomplished only in the context of communion, however, as personhood always seeks communion[42] and at the same time transcends the limits of creation. Personal presence is fully realized in the communion of the Church.

Because post-modernity is fundamentally existential, Zizioulas recognizes that we must urgently interpret the Gospel in existential

---

[40] J.D. ZIZIOULAS, *Communion and Otherness*, 219. See also C. P. SCHROEDER, *Suffering Toward Personhood: John Zizioulas and Fyodor Dostoevsky In Conversation On Freedom and the Human Person*, 260. Schroeder comments that the sought after friend is therefore present, even in being absent. Furthermore, the others in the café are understood as absent even in their presence insofar as they are defined by physical boundaries, and not in terms of relationship; as they are present only as objects of perception and not as persons.

[41] Ibid., 216.

[42] Cf. J.R. MEYER, *An Ek-static View of the Person*, 122.

terms[43] so to truly and deeply Christianize the world. The person always desires to go outside of his or her self to define his or her self, but desires to maintain their particularity therein. The theological project of Zizioulas attempts to present the Church to the world as a complete response to these fundamentally human existential questions that seem to demand answers beyond traditional Western metaphysics. Zizioulas's attempts to answer these questions are described by him as using a maximalist ecclesiology, in which the Church is a model against which we measure how we understand and live in communion with the other.[44] To attempt to define the person as relational with the use of the term *ecclesial hypostasis* is the task to which we now turn.

---

[43] Cf. J.D. ZIZIOULAS, *The Orthodox Church and the Third Millenium*, Sourozh, 2000, 24.

[44] Cf. J.D. ZIZIOULAS, *Communion and Otherness*, 241.

# Chapter Seven

# Metropolitan John Zizioulas: A Theological Search for the Human Person as Ontological and Relational

> Then Moses said to God, 'If I come to the sons of Israel and say to them, "The God of your fathers has sent me to you, and they ask me 'what is his name?' what shall I say to them?" God said to Moses, 'I AM WHO I AM." 'And he said, 'Say this to the sons of Israel, 'I am has sent me to you"
>
> (Exodus 3:13-14).

## 7.1 Athanasius of Alexandria: Truth as *Logos*

The God who reveals to Moses as "I am" is first Trinitarian, and so all of theology should flow from this place of origin, the Trinitarian origin, beginning, in the East with *De Deo Trino*, unlike the West theologically proceeding from *De Deo Uno.*[1] Situating ourselves in early Trinitarian doctrine, Athanasius of Alexandria and the Cappadocian Fathers assist in facilitating the understanding that God is first Three before he is One. To combat the heresy of Arianism, the Church needed a revision of the traditionally Greek *logos* approach to truth. Zizioulas recognizes that the Alexandrian theologian Athanasius (296-373), the chief Patristic Father and

[1] R. CANTALAMESSA, *Contemplating the Trinity,: The Path to the Abundant Christian Life,* Word Among Us, 2007, 13-14.

defender of Trinitarianism against Arianism, was instrumental in maintaining the doctrine of the *logos* but only under the condition that the *logos* is identical with the Son and so is part of the Trinity.[2] The Son's being belongs to the substance of God, while the world's being belongs to the will or love of God. First, by linking the being of the Son absolutely with the substance of the Father, Athanasius, departs from Greek *logos* ontology and embraces the Christian ontology influenced by the Eucharistic thinking of Ignatius and Irenaeus.[3] It is accomplished by connecting the existence of Christ with the substance of the Father, which leads to the view that substance possesses almost by definition a relational character.[4] Simply put, if God's being is by nature relational, and if it can be signified by the word 'substance', then the idea of substance has been radically transformed and employed in a Christian manner. This Christian understanding leads to the conclusion that, *to be* is not the same as *to will* or, hence, as *to act.*[5] Walter Cardinal Kasper, speaking of the metaphysical importance of the dogma that links divine substance to the eternal person of the Son, observes that it also leads to a revolution in the understanding of being. It is not substance that is ultimate and supreme, but relation. To put it in more concrete terms: *love is the all determining reality* and the meaning of being.[6]

---

[2] Cf. J.D. ZIZIOULAS, *Being As Communion*, 83.

[3] Ibid., 84.

[4] Ibid.

[5] Ibid.

[6] W. KASPER, *Theology and Church*, Crossroads, London, 1989, 29-30.

## 7.2 Athanasius of Alexandria: God's Substance and His Will

Secondly, because of the connection between existence and substance, Athanasius makes a subsequent distinction between God's substance and his will. Through this, a proper distinction between God and the world was achieved. The Greek mind could continue to identify God with being but was no longer obliged to link his being to the world because of ontological necessity.[7] Athanasius does not abandon ontological thought, according to Zizioulas, but raises it to the level its nature requires.[8] When Athanasius' language was adopted at the Council of Nicaea, Greek *monism* was officially overcome through the Christianization of the term 'substance', which takes on a meaning in Christianity which is entirely different from that found in Greek thought precisely because of relations within the Triune God. However, the Council of Nicaea had yet to make a distinction between the terms *ousia* and *hypostasis.*[9]

## 7.3 The Cappadocian Father Saint Basil the Great: Ousia and Hypostasis

For the Cappadocian Fathers, we find that the Fatherhood of God was a point of departure and that the natural understanding of personhood was understood as insufficient. The Cappadocian

---

[7] Cf. J.D. Zizioulas, *Being As Communion*, 84.

[8] Ibid.

[9] See First Ecumenical Council of Nicaea, DH #126, *vel ex alia substantia aut essentia.*

Father Saint Basil the Great of Caesarea (330-379) in his *Letters*, addresses the difference between substance and person in reference to the Holy Trinity. Basil begins by making a distinction between *ousia* and *hypostasis*. Basil speaks of those who presume to make no distinction between the terms 'substance' and 'person'[10] in reference to the Holy Trinity. He uses the example of how the Bible describes the person of Job to illustrate his point.[11] Basil laments the use of the general term 'man' to describe the substance of the human alone and not the person. For Basil, the use of the term "man" is insufficient because it fails to individuate, and particularity is necessary for participation in the created order. Basil states, "For, because of the indefiniteness of the term, he who says 'man' has introduced through our hearing some vague idea, so that although his nature is manifested by the name, that which subsists in the nature and is specifically designated by the name is not indicated."[12] Referring to the description of the person of Job in Scripture, Basil states:

> However, as to the description of the substance, nothing is said, since it makes no contribution to the proposed object of the discourse; but the 'certain' one is characterized by specific marks, such as situation, traits of character, and the external characteristics which serve to differentiate him and set him apart from the general notion. Consequently, by all

---

[10] Cf. BASIL, *Letter 38*: *To His Brother Gregory, Concerning the Difference between Substance and Person*, in *The Fathers of the Church*, R.J. Deferrari, ed, New York, 1951, 84.

[11] Ibid.

[12] Ibid.

> these means—the name, the place, the particular qualities of the soul, and the exterior characteristics seen in him—a clear description is made of the man whose story is given. On the other hand, if the meaning of substance were being given, there would have been no mention of the aforesaid matters in the explanation of its nature.[13]

Therefore, that which is spoken of in the specific sense pertains to person, or *hypostasis*, according to Basil. Notably, Basil's understanding of the divine person finds in the human an example which does not separate human understanding of personhood from divine personhood but on the contrary more deeply links the two. Basil affirms this by declaring: "You will not err if you transfer to divine doctrines this principle of differentiation between substance and person which you have recognized in their relation to human affairs."[14] Human understanding of person is therefore different in Basil from what it is in the West, for Basil understands the human person through a simple relationship and distinction between substance and person. Perhaps, in our opinion, we may consider reintroducing in the theological West Basil the Great as a point of departure for our understanding of personhood.

Zizioulas regards the Cappadocian contribution of Saint Basil the Great as a critical theological position. He is convinced that "philosophy can arrive at the confirmation of the reality of the person,

---

[13] Ibid., 86.

[14] Ibid.

but only theology can treat of the genuine, the authentic person."[15] The treatment of substance within Basil's theology leads Zizioulas to the conclusion that "substance never exists in a 'naked' state, that is, without *hypostasis*, without a 'mode of existence."[16] Zizioulas's position is not far from David Walsh, as Walsh also is of the opinion that the substance based categories insufficiently attempt to define personhood. The theological determination of person found in Saint Basil the Great and Zizioulas thus finds commonality with Walsh, yet Walsh does not posit that even a divine determination of personhood is able to render it definable, as it always remains unfathomable mystery.

[15] J.D. ZIZIOULAS, *Being As Communion*, 43.

[16] Ibid., 41. See A. SICARI, "Communio in Henri DeLubac", Communio US, Vol. 19, 1992, 450-464 for an insight into how this approach to substance assists in responding to the argument of K. Barth and E. Brunner that communion can only take place with a person, a subject, Christ, and not with sacred means. Sicari states: "One can reply that primitive objective sense precisely demands the acknowledgement of two facts: that the communion of believers is realized in history by means of objective and efficacious signs instituted by Christ himself; and that this objective sacramental participation must have within itself, within its center, something personalist, worthy of personal subjects for whom it is destined. One could not establish the realism of Christ's personal presence in the Eucharist on anything better than this."

## 7.4 *Hypostasis* as Conferring Ontology

Based on this principle Zizioulas constructs a general theological methodology which he roots in his understanding of the Greek Patristic Fathers:

> The basic ontological position of all of the theology of the Greek Fathers may be set out briefly as follows. No substance or nature exists without person or hypostasis or mode of existence. No person exists without substance or nature, *but* the ontological 'principle' or 'cause' of being, i.e. that which makes a thing to exist, is not the substance or nature but the *person* or *hypostasis.* Therefore being is traced back not to substance but to person.[17]

This position enables Zizioulas to argue that outside of the Trinity there is no God and no divine substance.[18] Since personhood in the Greek world had no ontological content but was something merely accidental (like a mask worn in the theatre), the Christian East not only inherited the problem that the term *prosopon* lacks ontological content but also the problem of there being no distinction between *ousia* and *hypostasis.*[19] The Christian East in the first

---

[17] J.D. Zizioulas, *Being As Communion*, 42, note 37.

[18] Ibid., 41.

[19] See Athanasius, *Letter to the bishops of Egypt and Libya*, (PG. 25, 1036 B). Cf. J.D. Zizioulas, *Being As Communion*, 36. "The term 'hypostasis' never had any connection with the term 'person' in Greek philosophy. As we have seen, 'person' would have been regarded by the Greeks as

centuries spoke of the three *hypostases* in God,[20] because they understood that the persons have ontological content. However, according to Zizioulas, because of a lack of terminological distinction, the precise meaning would have been that there were three separate substances in God. Zizioulas maintains that this lack of identification between substance and *hypostasis* is what led to the Trinitarian disputes of the 4th century. For example, he argues that since the time of Tertullian, the term 'person' had been used in the West for the three persons in the Holy Trinity: *una substantia, tres personae.*[21] The East would not accept this, however, because they believed it led to Sabellianism which is the belief that God manifests himself in merely three separate roles, or masks.[22] According to Zizioulas, it was thus necessary to find a mode of expression that would give ontological content to each person of the Holy Trinity, thus avoiding Sabellianism, and at the same time not endangering monotheism or the absolute ontological independence of God in relation to the world.[23]

Zizioulas notes that the gradual divergence of the term *hypostasis* from *substance* led to the momentous step, achieved by the

---

expressive of anything but the essence of man, whereas the term 'hypostasis' as already closely linked with the term 'substance' and finally was identified fully with it."

[20] See ORIGEN, *Commentary on St. John's Gospel, II*, 6 *Commentary on the Gospel According to John*, in *The Fathers of the Church*, (V.80). Cf. J.D. ZIZIOULAS, *Being As Communion*, 37.

[21] TERTULLIAN, *Against Praxeas*, 11-12 (PL 2, 1670D). See J.D. ZIZIOULAS, *Being As Communion*, 37.

[22] Cf. J.D. ZIZIOULAS, *Being As Communion*, 37.

[23] Ibid.

Cappadocian Fathers, of the identification of *hypostasis* with the term *prosopon.*[24] He notes that such identification of the existential term 'person' with the ontological term *hypostasis* was revolutionary and seems to have escaped the attention of historians of philosophy.[25] Thus, for Zizioulas, the introduction of an existential or human term to make a necessary Trinitarian distinction has universal metaphysical import.[26] Essentially, to-be and to-be-in-relation become identical. For Zizioulas, the relational category of person has no ontological content outside of theology, for it is dependent on its connection with the ontological term *hypostasis* (which is now connected with person rather than with substance), understood in a Trinitarian context, for its ontology. This therefore necessitates the philosophical conclusion, illuminated by theology, that being is dependent upon personhood, relational and ontological personhood, for its ontological status. Zizioulas describes the convergence of the two terms in a two-fold thesis:

a) The person is no longer an adjunct to a being, a category which we *add* to a concrete entity once we have first

---

[24] Ibid.

[25] Ibid., 39.

[26] See A. LOUTH, *Maximus the Confessor*, New York, 1996, 51. Louth here describes the distinction between *hypostasis* and nature in a Trinitarian context that is achieved in the Cappadocian Fathers and is used even more widely by St. Maximus the Confessor, especially in his understanding of his distinction between *logos* and *tropos* as a parallel to the distinction between *ousia* and *hypostasis*, the first category in both being at the level of being *ousia*, and the second being at the level of a "mode of existence," *hypostasis*.

verified its ontological hypostasis. It is itself the hypostasis of the being.

b) Entities no longer trace their being to being itself, that is, being is not an absolute category in itself, but to the person, to precisely that which *constitutes* being, that is, enables entities to be entities. In other words from an adjunct to a being (a kind of mask) the person becomes the being itself and is simultaneously a most significant point, the constitutive element (the 'principle' or 'cause') of beings.[27]

Comparatively for David Walsh the person is "before being" and "beyond being." The person cannot be defined within being. For Walsh, the person in God is the "encompassing ontology."[28]

## 7.5 The *Hypostasis* of the Father as Creator of all Being

Zizioulas, in this regard, regards the communion between God and the human person because of the freedom of the person of the Father to create out of love, and not out of the necessity of substance.[29] With the Father

[27] J.D. Zizioulas, *Being As Communion*, 39.

[28] D. WALSH, *Politics of the Person as the Politics of Being*, Introduction,, 12-13.

[29] Cf. J.D. Zizioulas, *Being As Communion*, St. Vladimir Seminary Press, 1997, 44. See P.G. Renczes, S.J. Doctoral Dissertation Director of our Second Project (*Personhood and Communion: A Critical Application of Relational Ontology in Ecclesiology*, Blessed Hope, 2018) See his *Agir De Dieu et Liberté de L'Homme*, Paris, 2003, 56-57, for an understanding of

and from the Father ontology and otherness is given in creation. Based in Maximus, this understanding of creation determines the anthropological truth that the only exercise of freedom in an ontological manner is love.[30] Again here we find convergence of a philosophical and theological search for personhood. What could possibly happen if a Trinitarian notion, as opposed to a philosophically substance based understanding of God prevailed?[31]

The second leavening, therefore, which is a result of the existential and ontological convergence is when the being of God himself was identified with the person of the Father, for Zizioulas attributes to Basil the Great the identification of the cause of God's being and life as the *hypo-stasis*, the person of the Father.[32] In Basil, the one God is with the Father of Jesus Christ and the *spirator* of the Holy Spirit, making the Trinity ontologically dependent upon the person of the Father and not upon its own substance. Zizioulas thinks that this understanding is closest to the biblical conception of faith in the Trinity and thus suggests that it provides the best possibility for dialogue with other monotheistic faiths.[33] A *person* must create, not a *substance*. Raniero Cardinal Cantalamessa notes the Eastern Fathers

---

how Maximus the Confessor transforms from the inside the Aristotelian understanding of God as the Prime Mover, retaining Aristotelian categories, yet at the same time transforming them.

[30] J.D. ZIZIOULAS, *Being As Communion*, 46.

[31] H. U. Von BALTHASAR, *Cosmic Liturgy: The Universe According to Maximus the Confesso*r Ignatius Press, 2003, 216. For Aristotle the highest and most comprehensive category of being was *ousia*, the existing essence.

[32] Ibid., 40.

[33] See J.D. ZIZIOULAS, *Communion and Otherness*, 154.

proceeded from the divine *Persons*, rather than from the concept of nature. In the Trinity, Cantalamessa notes, each Person identifies with the other, giving himself to the other, and sustains the existence of the other. Building on the Eastern doctrine of *perichoresis* in the Trinitarian doctrine, which is the "interdependence of persons," Cantalamessa argues that this may apply to more of an understanding of "the unity of activity within the Three toward one another."[34]

## 7.6 The *Hypostasis* of the Human Person in the Church

Notwithstanding the great achievements in the modern philosophical movement, one of its greatest flaws, despite all of its gains toward personhood, is in the denial of the Fall, and this theological reality, we argue with Zizioulas, must be accepted. This is precisely why modern philosophy needs theology. Zizioulas argues that Patristic theology requires a theological interpretation of person. Therefore, from a Patristic perspective, the person is understood according to two modes of existence, as a *biological hypostasis* and as an *ecclesial hypostasis.*[35] Regarding the *biological hypostasis*, the human is a tragic failure and needs an ontology beyond nature.[36] Humans cannot affirm their *hypostasis* with ontological freedom, because they subsist as necessity. They possess both *eros* and a body,

[34] R. CANTALAMESSA *Contemplating the Trinity: The Path to the Abundant Christian Life,* Word Among Us Press, 2007, 17.

[35] Cf. J.D. ZIZIOULAS, *Being As Communion*, 50.

[36] Ibid., 53.

but both are only in the context of natural limitations.[37] Zizioulas is not entirely ambivalent toward human nature, as some of his critics have suggested.[38] However, he nevertheless remains very critical about the ontological limitations of human nature. We for one to hold the same position as Zizooulas that *eros*, leads to death. *Eros*, according to our understanding, leads to communion, which must become ontological to be enduring into eternity. Zizioulas, nevertheless, while highlighting these limitation of nature, directs us toward the possibility of theology giving a defining meaning to personhood.

The *biological hypostasis* is the person without the Church, and is entirely bound up with being subject to death.[39] Humans bound by nature attempt to raise their freedom on a natural level of ontological absoluteness, which if chosen, Zizioulas argues, leads only to *nihilism.*[40] Furthermore, the b*iological hypostasis,* or the person without the Church, tends toward individualism or separation of the *hypostases*, which ultimately ends in nothing other than death. While seeking to acquire identity by way of nature alone, the *biological hypostasis*, Zizioulas states: "In its attempt to affirm itself as hypostasis (it) discovers that finally its 'nature' has led it along a false path toward death."[41] He illustrates how the *eros* of the *biological*

---

[37] Ibid.,52-53.

[38] See N.V. HARRISON, *Zizioulas on Communion and Otherness*, St. Vladimir Theological Quarterly, V.42, 1998, 285.

[39] Cf. J.D. ZIZIOULAS, *Communion and Otherness*, 219.

[40] Cf. J.D. ZIZIOULAS, *Being As Communion*, 50-51.

[41] Ibid., 51.

*hypostasis* is a desire for true transcendence, but falls short because of the limitations of nature:

> The biological constitution of the human hypostasis, fundamentally tied as it is to the necessity of its 'nature,' ends in the perpetuation of this 'nature' through the creation of bodies, that is, of hypostatic unities which affirm their identity as *separation* from other unities or 'hypostases.' The body, which is born as a biological hypostasis, behaves like the fortress of an ego, like a new 'mask' which hinders the hypostasis from becoming a person, that is, from affirming itself as love and freedom. The body tends toward the person, but leads finally to the individual.[42]

Personhood is described by Zizioulas as something to which the *biological hypostasis* needs to transcend. Humans are therefore in need of a basic constitutional change. According to Zizioulas, they are in need of a new birth into enduring personhood, not simply a moral improvement. A new mode of existence, which does not

---

[42] Ibid. "The body tends toward the person". Zizioulas means here that the body tries to lead to communion, such as in the example of the creation of language, speech, conversation, art and kissing, but at the same time it is always the "mask of hypocrisy, the fortress of individualism, the vehicle of the final separation, death." For him, the tragedy of the biological constitution of man's *hypostasis* does not lie in his not being a person because of it; it lies in his tending towards becoming a person through it and failing. Again, we do not hold the same position, as *eros* begins in the practical, the ethical, and must lead to the ontological to have enduring and eternal value.

abandon the body, is called for, an existence that overcomes inherently tragic elements of nature and retains what makes the person be - love, freedom and life.[43] What emerges with Maximus and Zizioulas is a mutual interdependence in love more deeply understood, so that the unique *logoi* of every created creature is more deeply appreciated as the other.[44] As a *microcosm of* the universe,[45] every *logoi* contains within itself the principle of all creation due its participation in the eternal *Logos.*

## 7.7 OTHERNESS AS ONTOLOGICAL

The other is more present to me than I am to myself. We are defined by the other. The other is necessary for our ontology. Zizioulas therefore provides an ontology that the West does not seem to adequately provide. We only need to look to Mother Theresa of Calcutta's love for the poor, or to the Parable of the Good Samaritan in the Gospel of Luke. If we pass by Christ in the poor we actually violate ourselves. Pope Francis emphasized this clearly in his Pontificate as well, one cannot walk by the person in need and assume to continue to maintain their Christian dignity, as the other constitutes their very being.

---

[43] Ibid., 53.

[44] See A. RIOU, *Le Monde Et L'Église Selon Maxime Le Confesseur*, 145 for an opinion that in the theology of Maximus, God's plan is to take up the natural differences of his creatures into a unity by the mystery of sonship in Christ and the Church.

[45] MAXIMUS THE CONFESSOR, *Ambigua* 7, *The Cosmic Mystery of Jesus Christ*, Saint Vladimir Press, Crestwood, NY, 3003, 45-74.

# Chapter Eight

# Metropolitan John Zizioulas: The Eucharist and Personhood; Life and Knowledge

"He who does not love does not know God; for God is love."

(1 John 4:8)

## 8.1 The Holy Eucharist as Epistemological Locus

From the foundation provided by Professor Betz in Part Two Chapter Four, one can see how the Eucharistic celebration would be the primary place where this ontological relationship of the human person to the divine person of the Son is realized and rediscovered. Following Betz, we are invited to discover the reception of the Tradition as intensely personal, as it is received by the human person within the dynamic event of the Holy Eucharist, which provides the person simultaneously with both ontology and knowledge. This occurs is a deeply spiritual manner as each person is an active participant in the Sacred Liturgy. This dynamic is then capable of being enhanced by listening and reflecting deeply on Sacred Scripture, the prayers of the Mass from the Roman Missal, the words of the priests applying the Gospel to their daily life, and the words and gestures of the Eucharistic Prayer itself as instructions for how to relate to others and enter into dialogical communion with both God and each other. It is in the heart of the Eucharistic community where a mystic is born.

Furthermore, with the help of Zizioulas, we have made the necessary discovery that the Eucharistic Liturgy is a place only defined by the glory of the future, where we find ourselves glorified and living in the fullness of the truth of our person. It is here that the original Tradition, the three Divine Persons, the Holy Trinity, pour collectively into the human person as a subject and recipient of Revelation, becoming in freedom the fullness of the person whom he or she is called to be.

It has been our experience that truth cannot be understood as abstract, for if it is, it will not take root in the integrated moral life of the person. If each person is a unique recipient of God's Self-Revelation, where does this Revelation occur? Where is it received? Metropolitan Zizioulas finds in the writings of Ignatius of Antioch that the idea of truth is not primarily a matter of epistemology in the strict sense of the word, but is connected with what we might call *life.*[1] Essentially, Zizioulas implicitly discovers that truth is found

[1] J.D. Zizioulas, *Being As Communion*, 78. It should be undisputed that such an understanding is found in the letter of Ignatius of Antioch, where Christ is often understood as the giver of life. Cf. Ignatius of Antioch, *Letter to the Magnesians 1:2,* Ancient Christian Writers, 69; Jesus Christ our enduring life; *Letter to the Ephesians*, 3:2, 61 "Jesus Christ our inseparable life"; *Letter to the Ephesians* 7:2, Here Ignatius states that God became man, true life in the face of death; 20:2 "Show obedience with undivided mind to the bishop and the presbytery, and to break the same Bread, which is the medicine of immortality, the antidote against death,

not in in theory, but in ethics, the ethics of life. An essential premise of this project, that ethics precedes ontology, is the fact that truth is found neither in abstract and theoretical principles, nor in concepts limited by nature alone, but only in a place where truth is able to be transmitted in a manner not limited by nature, and that place of encounter with truth is the Eucharistic Liturgy, and the personal meditative prayer that follows the Eucharistic Liturgy in the theological heart and mind of the Church. Yet, even here we encounter diverse methods and perspectives, yet to feel another's pain is to place ourselves in the other, and how could this occur in a place greater than the Holy Eucharist?

## 8.2 Pastoral Illustration – You are Necessary!

Recently, we were made privy to a pastoral conversation of a priest with a person seeking the spiritual life in the Catholic Church. As the priest spoke to the person, he found it necessary to share with her his new discovery that every person is "necessary." He therefore shared emphatically with this spiritual seeker the following: "You are Necessary!" The priest found that the acceptance of this objective truth to be life-changing for him in his discovery of being loved, and in sharing God's love with others, and he wanted to share this objective and subjective truth with the woman with whom he was conversing. If each person does indeed carry the whole, something essential is missing when that one person is not present, and this

---

and everlasting life in Jesus Christ"; *Letter to the Smyrnaeans* 4:1, "Jesus Christ our true life".

priest, many years in the priesthood had indeed found both an objective and subjective discovery, that now may be life changing for the person with whom this illuminating insight was shared.

## 8.3 Saint Ignatius of Antioch

We have found that the foundation for this manner of thinking is found in the life of the early Church, particularly in the Church Father Ignatius of Antioch, who combines knowledge with life and directs us more clearly towards an ontological approach to truth.[2] We have found that the fundamental natural desire for authentic communion and fellowship must be completed and fulfilled only in the context of a truth that overcomes the limitations of nature, and thus is eschatological, and Zizioulas has helped us understand that this truth is realized and discovered only in the context of communion.[3] Ignatius of Antioch, therefore, was able to achieve an understanding of truth that would have meaning for a person of Greek

---

[2] J.D. Zizioulas, *Being As Communion*, 79.

[3] Ibid.,17. Zizioulas affirms that this ontology "comes out of a Eucharistic experience of the Church." "The being of God is a relational being: without the concept of communion it would not be possible to speak of the being of God. It would not be impossible to speak of the 'one God' before speaking of the God who is 'communion,' that is to say, of the Holy Trinity. The Holy Trinity is a primordial ontological concept and not a notion which is added to the divine substance or rather which follows it, as is the case of the dogmatic manuals of the West, and alas, in those of the East in modern times".

mentality, without distorting the message of the Bible.[4] The Greek mind would have only been able to understand truth ontologically, unable to make this essential connection between ethics, or the practical life, and truth.[5] The Christian, on the other hand, must say *being* and *life* at the same time.[6] For Zizioulas, if truth is connected with Christ and salvation, it must be understood as communion,[7] which means that it must be discovered in the context of life.[8] Because of the Greek philosophical contribution, communion, which must be discovered in life if it is to be truly Christian, must also be understood as simultaneously ontological.[9]

---

[4]Ibid., 72. The Greek Fathers to whom Zizioulas most frequently makes reference are Irenaeus and St. Ignatius of Antioch.

[5] Ibid., 79.

[6] Ibid.

[7] Ibid., 110. Here Zizioulas identifies two types of Christology. The first identifies Christ as an individual. The second, however, involves a true ontology of communion. "When we make the assertion that He is the truth, we are meaning His *whole personal existence*, in this second type of Christology; that is we mean *His relationship* with His body, the Church, ourselves".

[8] Ibid., 81, 108-112. Cf. 79 to see how Zizioulas is critical of the Western understanding of being, which he observes is predicated on the philosophy of Aristotle, whom he believes holds that life is diminished to a "quality added to being, and not being itself". He continues by stating, "the truth of being is not found in life, but proceeds it".

[9] Ibid., 29. Zizioulas accepts the fundamental contribution in Greek philosophy regarding the ontological nature of being. However, he is clear to distinguish at the same time the problems of Greek philosophy. Zizioulas posits that consistently in Greek thought, from the Presocratics to the Neoplatonists, God is understood to be dependent upon the world, and the freedom of the Father to create is negated.

## 8.4 The Communion of Divine Persons and The Communion of Human Persons

The Eucharist, while it is the *locus* for the discovery of this epistemology also serves as the locus for an ontology of communion, as it will simultaneously illumine the mystery of the communion, with its foundation in the context of the Trinitarian communion of persons.[10] More explicitly, the discovery of truth in the Eucharistic Liturgy in the context of the Eucharist is to discover our Trinitarian God first as a communion of persons and not first as a substance. Zizioulas notes:

> If we believe in a God who is primarily an individual, who first *is* then *relates*, we are not far from a sociological understanding of *koinonia*; the Church in this case is not in her being communion, but only secondarily i.e. for the sake of her *bene esse*. The doctrine of the Trinity acquires in this case a decisive significance: God *is* Trinitarian; He is a relational being by definition; a non-trinitarian God is not koinonia in

---

[10] Cf. R.D. Turner, *Foundations for John Zizioulas' Approach to Ecclesial Communion*, Ephemerides Theological Lovanienses, December 2002, 439. If reference to this discovery of Zizioulas, Turner states, "The Church is not simply an institution, rather she is a 'mode of existence,' a way of being. The mystery of the Church, even in its institutional dimension, is deeply bound to the being of man, to the being of the world, and to the being of God". Cf. 438, where Turner speaks of one of the foundations to the ecclesiology of Zizioulas as being ontological.

his very being. Ecclesiology must be based on Trinitarian theology if it is to be an ecclesiology of communion.[11]

As seen here, the Church, understood as the place where the communion of persons is fully realized in a supernatural manner, actually has its birth and source in the life of the Holy Trinity, as this gives rise to an understanding that human personhood is brought about by God and remains in being because of the initiative of God.

## 8.5 Lex Orandi Lex Credendi

"The law of prayer is the law of belief." Could this principle also not be analogously applied to the relationship between philosophy and theology, with philosophy being analogous to the *orandi,* and theology analogous to the *credendi*? Furthermore, the Holy Eucharist, where this principle is realized insofar as it is historical, is dependent on the eschatological, and in the same manner as philosophy is dependent on theology, so too the historical is dependent on the eschatological in the event of the Holy Eucharist. We conclude that the Eucharistic Liturgy provides the historical

---

[11] J.D. Zizioulas, *The Church As Communion* (Keynote Lecture given at the World Council of Churches Fifth World Conference on Faith and Order, Santiago de Compostela, Spain, 3-14 August, 1993), St. Vladimir's Theological Quarterly 38, vol. 1, 1994, 3-16 (at 6). Cf. J.D.Zizioulas, "The Nature of the Unity We Seek: The Response of the Orthodox Observer", One in Christ,, St. Vladimir's Orthodox Press, New York, Vol 24, 1988, 343-353, 348. In an address to the Lambeth Conference of Anglican bishops, Zizioulas offered his theological assessment of their conclusions, and commenting in his address on the theme of ecumenism and Christian unity, issued a warning that we cannot go on seeking unity by treating the Church as a fundamentally social institution.

(philosophy), but then the ontology is ethically lived out in the human person as a *logoi* participating in the one *Logos.* Ethics therefore leads to ontology (theological) which must be informed by the future (eschatology) so that it bears a proper truth based ontology from the future (Zizioulas), but ontology must then again lead back to ethics, which is the ecclesial life lived out in action and development of the moral life.

## 8.6 Corporate Personhood and *Societas*

Even while Zizioulas asserts that the Church needs to give people an enduring and eschatological anthropology which will justify them as true persons, he realizes that the modern political person lives under the weight of the opposition between the individual and the collective, whose social life is understood in the context of *societas* rather than of *communio.*[12] Modern Democracy does have the resources to properly understand the exalted role of the particular person with respect to the whole of society. The Church must not manifest opposition between the individual and the collective, which is a characteristic only proper to *societas,* not to *communio.*[13] This may be applied to politics and serve as an luminary for politics. Each person is truly the center of the Universe, but at the same time the smallest, weakest and frailest must then be recognized with rights as an incalculable treasure. Zizioulas offers the concept of corporate personhood as a response to the problem of individualism.

---

[12] Cf. P. McPartlan, *The Eucharist Makes the Church: Henri De Lubac and John Zizioulas in Dialogue*, Eastern Christian Publications, PA, 2006, 138-139.

[13] Ibid.

He therefore develops an understanding of corporate personhood which is absolutely identified with the community of Christ in the celebration of the Eucharist, where the One and the Many are simultaneous.[14]

While corporate personhood appears only in a Eucharistic context for Zizioulas, it nevertheless theologically illumines the proper notion of both the individual and the communal from a political perspective. For example, in the Sacred Liturgy there is no opposition between the individual and the collective, and personhood is realized in the context of communion. Theologically, the person is not a means to an end, but in the context of the Sacred Liturgy, personhood is an end in itself because it is realized liturgically. Theologically, the Eucharist is the only place where individuals truly discover their identities as persons, as the Eucharist is an anti-individualistic act,[15] for, in the Eucharist, the human person ceases to become an individual and becomes a theological person, the *ecclesial hypostasis*;[16] Christ is the Corporate Person *par excellence*, as He in his own person is the collective corporate person.

British theologian, Zizioulas expert, and former Catholic University of America Professor, Paul McPartlan explains that: "We cannot be a person in relation to Adam because he is dead; his 'I' has expired." McPartlan continues: "But I can be a person in relation to

---

[14] Cf. J.D. ZIZIOULAS, *La Vision eucharistique du monde et l'homme contemporain*, Contacts, V. 19, St. Vladimir Orthodox Press, New York, 1967, 83-92.

[15] Ibid., 90.

[16] J.D. ZIZIOULAS, "The Pneumatological Dimension of the Church", Communio, US Vol, 1, 1993., 142.

Christ for he is Risen and lives; his 'I' is the undying uncreated 'I' of the Son."[17] Therefore, only through life in his Resurrection can the person of Christ be Corporate. Only Christ makes ontological and corporate personhood possible.

If we understand the discovery of truth in this manner, it not only makes all discovery of knowledge, or epistemology, dependent upon the Eucharistic event, but it makes all of history dependent on the Spirit and proves to be the solution to the perennial problem of ideology, materialism, and institutionalism, that has plagued Western thought. All truth, when understood in the context of the Trinity, will also then necessarily be discovered and realized in the context of the Holy Eucharist where the Holy Spirit provides a true synthesis of the historical and the eschatological, and by analogy also provides a synthesis of faith and reason.

## 8.7 Eschatology as Truth Bearing

Eschatology for Zizioulas is truth bearing, and the Holy Spirit brings about this truth eschatologically. For Zizioulas, with a proper eschatology, which is necessary for philosophy as well, the Holy Spirit turns living history into an actual presence.[18] The Eucharist for Zizioulas is therefore the paradoxical locus of the "memory of

---

[17] P.McPARTLAN, *The Eucharist Makes the Church.*

[18] J.D. ZIZIOULAS, "Apostolic Continuity And Orthodox Theology: Towards A Synthesis of Two Perspectives" Saint Vladimir's Theological Press , New York, Vol. 19, 1975, 75-108.83.

the future."[19] Here the Kingdom of God is present, as it is the fullness of theological transcendence, as the future actually visits history.[20] This is the mystery of presence and absence in personhood realized fully. The Eucharist thus becomes the moment when the Church realizes that her roots are found *simultaneously* in the past and in the future, in history and in the eschaton.[21] The human person, philosophically, is also by analogy immanent and transcendent. This concept introduces a theophanic, or metahistorical[22] contribution to the more traditional, or historically, based sequence of yesterday-today-tomorrow[23] that has tended to dominate Western

---

[19] J.D. ZIZIOULAS, *Remembering the Future*, Sebastian Orthodox Press, Banja, Serbia, 2023, 6. J.D. ZIZIOULAS, "Apostolic Continuity And Orthodox Theology: Towards A Synthesis of Two Perspectives", 83. Zizioulas makes reference here to the anaphora of the Liturgy of St. John Chrysostom. He also states that the Eucharistic paradox is something that no historical consciousness can ever comprehend.

[20] J.D. ZIZIOULAS, "Apostolic Continuity And Orthodox Theology: Towards A Synthesis of Two Perspectives", 106.

[21] Ibid., 91.

[22] Ibid., 75-76. Zizioulas comments, "On the one hand, Orthodoxy is known for its devotion Tradition. This makes history acquire decisiveness in the consciousness of the Orthodox Churches, which is thus oriented toward a past with respect and devotion. On the other hand, Orthodoxy is known for the centrality and importance which it attributes to worship in its life and theology, and this leads to a 'theophanic', and in a sense 'metahistorical' view of the Church. Deep in these two aspects of Orthodox consciousness lie the seeds of a duality, which could be easily turned into a dichotomy."

[23] Ibid., 84, 90. The synthesis of the historical and the eschatological is essentially the sacramental nature of the Church. The past and the future are viewed as one indivisible reality in the event of the Eucharist.

thinking. This relationship between tradition and worship, or history and eschatology, provides a methodology, in our opinion, for future ecclesiological discourse that is more person and spirit based than substance based.[24] Zizioulas states:

> The Spirit is the one who brings the eschatological into history, He confronts the process of history with its consummation, with its transformation and transfiguration. By bringing the eschatological into history the Spirit does not vivify a pre-existing structure; He *creates* one; He changes linear history into a *presence.*[25]

As the Sacred Liturgy is presence theologically, so the human person is presence philosophically. The eschatological determination of the Church, provides the contribution which preserves us from the danger of identifying the Church as merely a social

---

[24] Cf. J.D. ZIZIOULAS, *Eucharist, Bishop, Church*, Holy Cross Orthodox Press, Brookline, MA, 2007, 52-53. In this Zizioulas's Doctoral Dissertation at the University of Athens, the dynamic is realized in the recognition that the Book of Revelation and the celebration of the Eucharist have a very intimate relationship. According to Zizioulas, either the Book of Revelation influenced the Eucharist, or vice versa. With this understanding, there is a "mystical identification of the Church in heaven before the throne of God worshiping before the Table of the Eucharist". Zizioulas notes that particularly Chapters 4 and 5 of the Book of Revelation, "make no sense unless the eucharistic assembly incarnates on earth the very Church of God".

[25] J.D. ZIZIOULAS, "Apostolic Continuity And Orthodox Theology: Towards A Synthesis of Two Perspectives", 83.

institution, and simultaneously from viewing the Church in overly legalistic terms, as it may also assist us in reducing persons to a means, or toward the negation of their transcendence.[26] In referring to the dependence of the Church upon the Holy Spirit, and as we look forward to the unification of all Christians in one Eucharist, Zizioulas reminds us that this may only be accomplished by the Holy Spirit, and not by human action. Zizioulas continues by commenting:

> This means not only that human attempts at 'togetherness,' 'openness,' etc., cannot constitute the catholicity of the Church, but that no plan for a progressive movement toward catholicity can be achieved on a purely historical and sociological level.[27]

The metahistorical contribution of Orthodox theology to an understanding of communion, governed by eschatology and pneumatology, demands an understanding of communion that is absolutely dependent upon communion with God, and therefore not relegated to mere sociological and historical conceptions.[28] Thus, our desire

---

[26] J. D. ZIZIOULAS, "The Nature of the Unity We Seek: The Response of the Orthodox Observer", One in Christ, V. 24, 1988, 343. Here Zizioulas comments that the Orthodox approach to unity always being understood in the context of the Eucharist has helped to avoid problems such as clericalism, and the clash between charisma and institution.

[27] J.D. ZIZIOULAS, *Being As Communion*, 161.

[28] CF. C. GUNTON, , *The Promise of Trinitarian Theology*, Edinburgh, 1997, 56. In Chapter Four, entitled, "The Community, the Trinity and the Being of the Church," Gunton acknowledges here that there are

for Christian Unity may not be constructed with our own plans, but God must provide the plan.

A proper eschatology makes the structure of the Church as something necessary and unchangeable,[29] and therefore transcending purely human constructs. A proper eschatology provides protection from the historicism that seeks the fulfillment of the Kingdom in this world, through social construct, as has happened in tragic historical examples such as Nazi Germany. Zizioulas notes:

> In consequence of this pneumatological vision, the criteria for ecclesiality may not be derived solely from history but must depend also on this eschatological dimension of hope

---

sociological and historical conceptions of the Church which are viable, but that is just the first level of understanding the Church. But he says that at another level, "the question of the being of the Church is one of the most neglected topics of theology". Zizioulas uses the example of the Divine Liturgy of the Greek Orthodox Church to illustrate that the words of institution, and the entire *anamnetic* dimension of the Church, are placed at the disposal of the Spirit, as if they could not constitute in themselves a sufficient assurance of God's presence in history.

[29] CF. D. BATHRELLOS, *Church, Eucharist, Bishop: The Early Church in the Ecclesiology of John Zizioulas*, Chapter 8,133-145, in *The Theology of John Zizioulas.* Ed. D.H. Knight, Hampshire England, 2007, 140. Here Bathrellos challenges Zizioulas, in what he understands as a lack of a vision for potential changes in the structure of the Church; mentioning the fact that his overemphasis on structure creates a tension in his theological system. Bathrellos questions how such an existential approach is able to be reconciled with this emphasis on structure. Our position is to the contrary however, as we see this diffusion of the dichotomy placed between the existential and the institutional to be one of the greatest fruits of the theology of Zizioulas.

> and expectation which the Church embodies in our world. This kind of ecclesiology is very far from giving rise to the false hope, the opium, of a 'social gospel' according to which history leads, and is led by the Church, toward perfection in the form of progress or revolution.[30]

At the same time, however, the eschatological dimension protects the Church from being static, because of the proper pneumatology that necessarily accompanies eschatology. With a Eucharistic understanding of the Church, pneumatology and ecclesiology are understood as inseparable from eschatology and communion.[31] The proper integrated synthesis of these themes within ecclesiology provides the opening to understanding the possibility of the political person[32] that becomes fully realized and developed in the context of the ecclesial structure of the Church that is beyond history and

---

[30] J.D. ZIZIOULAS, "Informal Groups in the Church: An Orthodox Viewpoint", Papers of the Second Cerdic Colloquium, Strasbourg, Pittsburgh, 1971, 291.

[31] Cf. J.D. ZIZIOULAS, *Being As Communion*, 131. Here Zizioulas speaks of eschatology and communion as necessary aspects of pneumatology and ecclesiology, because they "constitute fundamental elements of the Orthodox understanding of the Eucharist."

[32] Cf. J D. BATHRELLOS, *Church, Eucharist, Bishop: The Early Church in the Ecclesiology of John Zizioulas*, Chapter 8. Cf. J.D. ZIZIOULAS, *The Early Christian Community, Origins to the Twelfth Century* in Christian Spirituality:, B. McGinn, J. Meyendorff, J. LeClerq eds, London, 1986, 43. Individualism is truly an existential dilemma, and here Zizioulas speaks of the Eucharistic Community as a place for the truly overcoming individualism. The deepest existential questions are only answered by ontology.

theory, and is "eschatological communion."[33] Without this eschatological dimension, persons in the Church , and by analogy in society, may run the risk of being reduced to mere moral usefulness.[34]

## 8.8 The Icon and Eschatology as Epistemological

The Eastern Church places a high theological priority on the *icon* and the significance of the i*conostasis* liturgically. The theology of the icon depends absolutely on the proper understanding of the person as eschatological.[35] The value of the ontology of the *icon* is predicated entirely upon relation, the manner with which one thing

---

[33] Cf. J.D. ZIZIOULAS, *Being As Communion*, 131. Here Zizioulas speaks of eschatology and communion as necessary aspects of pneumatology and ecclesiology because they "constitute fundamental elements of the Orthodox understanding of the Eucharist". Continuing, in reference to eschatology and communion, "it is necessary to make these aspects of Pneumatology constitutive of *ecclesiology*. What I mean by 'constitutive' is that these aspects of Pneumatology must qualify the very ontology of the Church".

[34] Ibid., Zizioulas understands these examples to include such things as the creation of "moral examples useful to society, or to "serve the religious needs of man, who is looking for 'peace' 'prayerfulness' and so forth". Continuing, in the relation to a moral primacy, as opposed to an eschatological primacy in the Liturgy, "Simple, humble country chapels are preferred to light-filled cathedrals," "Episcopal liturgies are only for feasts", and "Vestments are simplified to be more humble ('moral' perfection demands it)". Zizioulas maintains that practices such as the kissing of priests hands, the touching of vestments to receive grace, and the kissing of holy icons and relics are to be preserved, but only through the understanding of "iconic symbolism".

[35] Ibid.,16.

refers to another.[36] This ontology accomplishes the relationship between history, or nature, and eschatology. If the eschatological understanding of person was not primary here, the practice of the veneration of the *icon* would be reduced to paganism.[37] It is our hope that if the theology of the *icon* is fully understood, we are provided not only with a theological approach to the Eucharist, but also the foundation for an adequate Christian epistemology, understood primarily in the context of the Eucharist by way of the ancient understanding of *sign*. The Eucharist is a *sign* insofar as not merely historical, but is more so eschatological, defined by what is to come and thus primarily in its whole as *sign*, as the Eastern understanding of the Divine Liturgy is primarily as an eschatological event. By our stating this, we by no means intend to reduce the truth of the full Real, Sacramental Presence of the person of Jesus Christ in the Eucharistic species. Furthermore, the nature of the Eucharist as a *sign* in its theological entirety has the capacity to inform and illumine the *polis* as well.

This epistemology, based in the theology of the *icon*, places the relational dimension as primary, understood through the theological understanding of the person. The Eucharist as eschatological presents us with the possibility of an *iconic* understanding of the truth. Pseudo-Dyonisius the Areopagite (5th or 6th Century AD)

[36] Ibid., 15.

[37] Ibid., 11 "The veneration of icons, the recognition of supernatural properties in holy relics, sacred vessels and objects and so forth can become forms of paganism, if these objects are regarded as possessing these properties *in their nature* and not in the personal presence of the saint to whom they are connected."

founds this epistemology in both a cataphatic and apophatic manner of knowledge and speaks of symbols and *icons* as windows to divine truth. The *icon* manifests truth as relational and protects it from being objectified because it is always defined by the future, thus eschatological. Truth is therefore rooted in the ontological and always needs ontology for the fullness of ethics. For Pseudo-Dyonisius the Areopagite, truth is only perceived and received through the mirror of relation, and relation must be ground in truth, not in a mere shadow, and that truth is ultimately the triune God.

For example, In Plato's "Allegory of the Cave," the prisoners confined to the cave could only see shadows on the wall, and thus understood only those shadows to be the truth. The real objects, however, were outside of the cave illumined by the sun. The only manner in which the prisoners are informed of the real truth is by one of the prisoners breaking free and then returning to the cave and informing the other prisoners of the reality occurring through real objects outside of the cave. The shadows on the wall reflect an approach to truth formed by nature alone, it therefore does not suffice. The shadow reveals only a partial truth, not the complete truth that only eschatology can reveal, and that is always mediated through the person. For Plato, the person of the one liberated prisoner is the mediator of truth to the other prisoners who remain bound by nature.[38]

If truth were merely ethical, the fellowship of the community would be invested with the power and the authority to determine truth, and the community alone is not invested with that power.

---

[38] See PLATO, *Republic*, Hackett Publishing, Cambridge, MA.,1992, and his "Allegory of the Cave."

Only the Eucharistic community is given that power because it is powered by the Holy Spirit who transcends the bounds of both nature and history, and thus is eschatological. Similarly in the political community the individual is not the sole arbiter of truth, but on the other hand is obliged to enter into the communion of the *polis* where truth is found.

Zizioulas emphasizes that the tragedy of the fallen condition is the priority of knowledge over love. A *post-lapsarian* epistemology determines that one can only love what one knows, since love comes out of knowledge. It is imperative, according to Zizioulas, that this tragic reality does not govern our understanding of metaphysical anthropology or, even less, of our approach to Trinitarian theology. For Zizioulas, a way of knowing through the *icon* serves to redeem and recover the priority of love not being reduced to knowledge.[39] Following the thought of Zizioulas, iconic epistemology may serve to further the concepts of relation, communion, and love, to be seen as primarily found in the Eucharistic Liturgy. The focus for an understanding of knowledge becomes understood in its theological fullness primarily in the reception of the mysterious reality of the other in the context of the Holy Eucharist, as opposed to the more individualistic approach to epistemology wherein the mind of the subject is engaged in an immediate analysis of the object presented, viewing it simply as an object before it has been received.

---

[39] J.D. ZIZIOULAS, *Being As Communion*, 104. Zizioulas argues that this reality, the priority of knowledge over love, is found in the theology of St. Thomas Aquinas.

In conclusion, Zizioulas further contributes to this *iconic* way of knowing, which places the Eucharist as a true paradigm of how humanity comes to knowledge and discovers truth in the context of communion, thus finding a true guiding light for how the political person may come to know within the community as well.

## 8.9 Parallel Lines in Contemporary Western Theology

For Zizioulas, an *iconic* way of knowing presents truth not as a product of the mind, but as a "visit", or a "dwelling."[40] The eschatological root of *iconic* knowledge, according to Zizioulas, "liberates truth from our 'conception,' 'definition,' 'comprehension' of it and protects it from being manipulated and objectified. It also makes it relational, in the sense that the truth of one being is able to be 'conceived' only in and through the mirror of another."[41] Notice, therefore, that with an acceptance of an *iconic* manner of knowing, that reception becomes prior to knowledge, and the other becomes necessary for the full reception of the truth, and as the truth is presented, the mystery is never exhausted.

In the West, for example, Professor Jean-Luc Marion is critical of basing a theological method upon the inherent link of God, being

---

[40] J.D. Zizioulas, *Being As Communion*, 100. This understanding of the iconological language of the Greek Fathers is understood, for Zizioulas, in the light of the primitive apocalyptic theology (i.e. the primitive Syro-palestinian tradition and is penetrated throughout the eucharistic liturgies of the East.)

[41] Ibid., and J.D. ZIZIOULAS, *Remembering the Future*, 137.

and thought.[42] The French Marion therefore responds to what he describes as an overly rational approach to theology in which the existential component is negated in favor of a metaphysical component that only understands God by way of the traditional manner as the being of beings.[43] Preserving the mystery is imperative for Marion, as he argues that substance metaphysics may be turned into a false idol.[44] According to Marion, the phenomenon of the absence of God in the world, which was an insight of the existential philosophy of Heidegger, must be taken seriously in our attempts to understand God. To this end Marion suggests maintaining complete silence before the face of God, in order to discover who God is. Orthodox theologian Aristotle Papanikolaou observes that this approach gives both Marion and Zizioulas the opportunity to go beyond a more traditional metaphysics of substance toward a Trinitarian theology of relationality and personhood.[45]

Now that the we have presented the philosophical and theological foundation for the mystery of personhood, and firmly established that a proper ontology is necessary for its full realization, we can now turn to the ethical dimension of how personhood is realized in the context of life, embracing the concept of the person bearing the mystery within his or her self as he or she journeys toward the

---

[42] A. PAPANIKOLAOU, *Being With God: Trinity, Apophaticism, and Divine-Human Communion*, University of Notre Dame, 2006, 93.

[43] J.L. MARION, *The Idol and Distance, Five Studies*, New York, 2001, 18.

[44] IBID., xxxviii.

[45] A. PAPANIKOLAOU, *Being With God*, 93.

*eschaton* making moral choices along the way, in the context of communion.

# PART FOUR

## *CONCLUSIONS*

## *A PATH FORWARD FOR PERSONHOOD*

# Chapter Nine

# Professor David Walsh: The Freedom of the Liberal Person

"I appeal to you for my child, Onesimus, whose father I have become in my imprisonment. Formerly he was useless to you, but now he is indeed useful to you and to me. I am sending him back to you, sending my very heart. So if you consider me your partner, receive him as you would receive me."

(The Letter of Paul to Philemon 10-12; 17)

## 9.1 The Russian Novel

We began as an undergraduate in the Department of Politics studying under the Irish born Professor David Walsh at the Catholic University of America. Professor Walsh presented to his graduate and undergraduate students that persons are both the origin and the end of politics; persons are the possibility of politics; that philosophy is political and the *polis* is philosophical. For Walsh, in the political community, the eschatological intersects with time.

At that time in the late 1990's, Professor Walsh had completed his first two books after his published Doctoral Dissertation. The books were, *After Ideology: Recovering the Spiritual Foundations of Freedom* (1990), and the *Growth of the Liberal Soul* (1997). The first book follows the aftermath of the totalitarian crisis of the 20th

Century. Walsh searched for the truth of the person emerging in the liberal order after the great tragedies of communism in the Soviet Republic and fascism in Europe.[1] These great ideological tragedies led to the cathartic rediscovery of personhood. It was a personhood foretasted in the great Russian novelist Fyodor Dostoyevsky (1821-1881) with the last of his great novels, *Brothers Karamazov*, with its rich development of personal characters unfolding in the great narrative of a philosophical drama in the late 19th Century, all before the rise of the totalitarian regime in the form of the Bolshevik Revolution of 1917, which Dostoyevsky foresaw, and which changed the trajectory of the history of that great nation.

We recall Walsh's introduction of the Russian philosophical novel, particularly through the reading of *Brothers Karamazov* in his classroom, so as to discover the greatness of multiple characters developing within a single novel so as to illumine the deep questions of the day to reflect the philosophical genius of a great author, who illumined personhood, and observed that every human person writes history his or her self, as the great protagonist, found within his or her choice for good or evil.[2] We found something greater in Walsh's classroom than what was happening on Capitol Hill, as we were introduced into the deeper philosophical dimension of politics, which helped us soar above the myopic political analysis of the day, and into the depths of the mystery of personhood.

Soaring like eagles, and buoyed by the guidance of this deeply spiritual political philosopher, who was piercing something greater

---

[1] D. WALSH, *After Ideology*, Harper San Francisco, 1990, 10-11.
[2] Ibid., 46-48.

than we ever imagined at that time, we looked deep into the history of the Catholic intellectual tradition to find the origins of liberal democracy, as Walsh provided us with a richly philosophical account of the potential that the latter had to offer the world. In 2009, at the time of our second project, we would have never expected, being so immersed in Greek Orthodox theology, that Walsh would provide us with the path back to the human person in a manner in which we never foresaw could be possible. As noted above, Professor Walsh took us back to the 15th Century where he found the origins and foundation of Christian politics in the form of a democratic republic with the Conciliarism of the German Cardinal and scholar Nicholas of Cusa (1401-1464), as we studied Cusa's efforts to reform the Holy Roman Empire and its relationship with the German States of the same Empire. Here we found the origins of what would be promoted in the first of the modern Popes, Leo XIII (1878-1903), who ushered the Catholic Church into the modern world by defending the dignity of the human person, particularly in his defining Social Encyclical *Rerum Novarum* (1891). In this modern encyclical on the human person Leo highlights the principles:

> Man alone among the animal creation is endowed with reason - it must be within his right to possess things not merely for temporary and momentary use, as other living things do, but to have and to hold them in stable and permanent possession; he must have not only things that perish in the use, but those also which, though they have been reduced into use, continue for further use in after time. This becomes still more clearly evident if man's nature be considered a little

> more deeply. For man, fathoming by his faculty of reason matters without number, linking the future with the present, and being master of his own acts, guides his ways under the eternal law and the power of God, whose providence governs all things. Wherefore, it is in his power to exercise his choice not only as to matters that regard his present welfare, but also about those which he deems may be for his advantage in time yet to come. Hence, man not only should possess the fruits of the earth, but also the very soil, inasmuch as from the produce of the earth he has to lay by provision for the future.[3]

In the wake of the Industrial Revolution beginning in Great Britain and extending to the United States, Leo turned to the dignity of rights to protect the rights of workers from being enslaved to their employer, thus protecting them from the evil ideology of Marxist materialism. This great contribution towards the dignity of the human person prepares the way for the theological work of the American Jesuit John Courtney Murray (1904-1967) whose work on personhood led to the great Declaration on Religious Liberty of the Second Vatican Council, *Dignitatis Humanae* (1965), which richly developed the rights of the human person based on the teaching of the modern popes, within the context of a constitutionally ordered society. The Pastoral Constitution on the Church, *Gaudium et Spes*, of the same year, 1965, emphasized the same methodology. We must necessarily remember as we go forward that at the heart of the

---

[3] LEO XIII, *Rerum Novarum*, Encyclical, 1891, # 6 and #7.

liberal construct is the recognition of the person as the inexhaustible center of value.[4]

## 9.2 The Emergence of the Liberal Person

The circle that began in undergraduate Political Theory at the Catholic University of America and was complemented by our nine years of post-graduate studies at the Pontifical Gregorian University in Rome, Italy, was made complete by Walsh as he placed an emphasis on political philosophers who were asking the same questions as we had asked, albeit notwithstanding the difference of our beginning from the standpoint of Revelation within the discipline of theology.

Now philosophically speaking, one first must appreciate the beginning of Liberalism in the thought of the English Thomas Hobbes (1588-1679), and John Locke (1632-1704), the French Jean-Jacques Rousseau (1712-1788), and the British John Stuart Mill (1806-1873). While these political philosophers did not have all of the answers, they were nevertheless asking the correct questions, as they implicitly and explicitly searched for personhood within the guiding light of the community. These great philosophers prefigured the birth of the American Republic in 1776, and the French Revolution of 1789, both giving emancipation to the human person within the political order.

Significant and influential political philosophers in the United States such as Ronald Dworkin (1931-2013) eventually followed.

[4] Ibid., 269-290.

Dworkin built on the philosophy of American political philosopher John Rawls (1921-2002). Dworkin argued that law may not be reduced to a mere set of rules, but rather involves principles and values that provide a moral framework for a body of people, thus signifying a morality that transcends the individual person. Walsh values these thinkers, as he has been deeply influenced by the political philosopher Eric Voegelin, and much appreciates the American political philosopher Leo Strauss (1899-1973), along with the German philosopher Hans-Georg Gadamer (1900-2002), each of whom sought the rejuvenation of liberal democracy based on their encounter with classical political philosophy. Furthermore, Walsh also appreciates and has studied deeply the contributions of the French Jacques Maritain (1882-1973), the Scottish-American philosopher Alasdair MacIntyre (1929-2025) and the Australian legal philosopher John Finnis (1940), all in the Thomist tradition of natural law and contributors to the argument. We must almost mention his appreciation for the British Michael Oakeshott (1901-1990), whom Walsh described as intellectually powerful in his reconceptualization of liberal ideas and practice in a form of Conservatism.[5]

Each one of these philosophers Walsh understood as a person seeking truth within the context of the community of persons, and each of these persons was to be valued in their search, inasmuch as he values his own contribution to this search. How would individual liberty be understood in the context of the civic virtue? Walsh asks this question in his *Growth of the Liberal Soul*, as the fragmentation

[5] D. WALSH, *Growth of the Liberal Soul*, University of Missouri Press, 1997, 57-59.

of the liberal democracy seeks to reconstruct itself from the ashes with transcendent moral principles.[6] For Walsh, the answers to these questions arise from the person being immersed in the *polis* themselves, as an approach to understanding these questions must incorporate the person in the context of community at the highest philosophical level.

## 9.3 The Church as the Theological Basis for Philosophical Communion

For philosophy to exist, one must be immersed within it, and when one is immersed within, one is never an isolated individual, but always a part of a political community which transcends and defines the individual. In this regard we see in Walsh's political philosophy the foreshadowing of the ecclesial person being immersed in the Eucharistic body of the Church. The person in the modern liberal political community radiates with particular luminosity, as does the ecclesial person, the *ecclesial hypostasis*, within the body of the Church. For Zizioulas, the person in the Church is immersed in his or her own particular reception of Revelation, and theology within the ecclesial Tradition. The baptized person, with ontological dignity, thus contributes to the life of the Church as a contributing believer, contemplating and reflecting upon the treasures of Catholic theology and participating actively in the life of the Church.

In the same way the person as citizen contributes to the life of the political community as a free subject, able to freely choose the

---

[6] Ibid., 237-276.

good, the true and the beautiful, and thus grow in virtue contributing to the life of the political community, which always transcends the citizen. For Walsh, each person is a unique recipient of God's Self-Revelation. For example, Walsh values each character developed in *Brothers Karamazov* insofar as each writes their own historical narrative, and each character is faced with the questions of life giving virtue or death ending vice, the choice of each character has infinite value, as the person carries the universal within his or her self.[7]

Being carried on the shoulders of these great thinkers preceding him, Walsh, in maintaining that ethics precedes ontology, understands that the language of rights is proper for ethics, as it properly emphasizes the horizon of the person, and that the priority of ethics does not abolish ontology. Insofar as freedom is understood properly in the context of the other, and the other is always understood in the political community as being closer to me than myself, than the language of rights is able to flourish in the context of a virtuous community.[8] If each person, according to Walsh, embraces the whole of reality, and "being" is actually understood by all to be "one person," then we have nothing to fear.[9] In fact, the only access to history, thus avoiding the historical dangers of nihilism and ideology, is through the lens of the human person, who both writes and analyzes history only through the rational lens of his or her same personhood.

---

[7] D. WALSH, *Politics of the Person as the Politics of Being*, Notre Dame Press 2016, 78-86, The individual exceeds the universal.

[8] Ibid., 44-45.

[9] Ibid, 123-155.

Liberal democracy, in fact, opens up new horizons for the person that a monarchical state could not provide, because in the latter, the free individual response with the totality of one's heart, mind and will, the response of the total person, as called for in the Dogmatic Constitution of the Church, *Dei Verbum*, was less possible. In a monarchical state, and prior to that in the Medieval state, the human person, we argue, was more constrained and thus less free to make individual moral choices that contributed to the development of his or her own personhood and the common good.

## 9.4 Human Rights as the Personalist Principle

American Papal Biographer of Pope Saint John Paul II, George Weigel, in his brilliant 2019 book, *The Irony of Modern Catholic History*, traces this path from the Pontificate of Pope Leo XIII through to the Pontificate of Pope Francis. Weigel credits Leo XIII with drawing on the essentially Thomistic convictions of law, freedom, Civil Society and the State, to pave the way for the personalist principle to emerge.[10] He describes the personalist principle as what we know today as the human rights principle, which maintains that all proper thinking about society, polity, culture, and economics begins with the intrinsic dignity of the individual human person, and not with the State, the political party, or the gender group.[11] Weigel understands this contribution of Pope Leo XIII to be the modern birth

---

[10] G. WEIGEL, *The Irony of Modern Catholic History: How the Church Rediscovered itself & Challenged the Modern World to Reform*, Basic Books, 2019, 80.

[11] Ibid., 148-152

of Christian Democracy, which understood that constitutionally ordered and popular self-government had its advantages for the development of the human person, as did the constitutional arrangements that kept a prudent distance between the institutions of the Church and the institutions of the State.[12] Weigel goes on to note that the pontificate of Leo XIII opened the Church to intellectual and cultural modernity.[13] Weigel then continues to describe the first six decades of the 20th Century as a period of great creativity in Catholic theology, now somewhat "unshackled" from some of the more institutional restraints prior to Pope Leo XIII. He refers to the value that *Ressourcemen*t (return to the sources) theology had for the renewal of theology in the Church as a whole, leading up to the Second Vatican Council.[14] He references the German Karl Adam (1875-1966) and Romano Guardini (1885-1968) as well as to the French Maurice Blondel (1861-1949) as being precursors to the *Ressourcement*, and the core of the movement being found in the French Dominicans Marie-Dominiqu Chenu, O.P. (1895-1990) and Yves Congar O.P. (1904-1995) along with the French Jesuit, Henri de Lubac (1896-1991).[15] The movement then gave rise to a push toward personalism and political theory, found in Catholic personalists such as the German Dietrich von Hildebrand (1889-1977) and Max Scheler

[12] Ibid., 76-84

[13] Ibid., 87.

[14] Ibid., 116.

[15] Ibid., 117-121.

(1874-1928),[16] The latter whose experimental phenomenology came to influence Karol Wojtyla in his second doctoral dissertation.[17]

As the American John Courtney Murray, S.J. (1904-1967) was the *peritus* of Francis Cardinal Spellman of New York at the Second Vatican Council, while Murray did not entirely influence the Council with his exact political theory, he contributed enough for the experience of vibrant American Catholicism under a particular Constitutional Democracy to be embraced by the Council Fathers, and in this embrace, Weigel reflects, the Fathers of the Council were able to disentangle themselves from the understanding that an alliance between the altar and throne or constitutional form of government, is essential for the Church's mission. Furthermore, Weigel notes, that due to the totalitarian regimes of the Twentieth Century, which must ever remain in the forefront of political thought, the Church must embrace the concept of religious freedom for the survival of the Church, for a totalitarian regime's desire to eliminate the public pronouncement of belief in God and of the Bible as an obstacle to human liberation, must be expunged, because of a violation of a truth which resides deep in the nature of the human person.[18]

Pope Saint John Paul II, in his Encyclical *Centesimus Annus* (1991), to commemorate one hundred years after *Rerum Novarum*, and to re-establish the same principles, followed a pattern established by Vatican II in *Gaudium et Spes*, advocating for a free and virtuous society that comprised of a dynamic interrelationship

---

[16] Ibid., 125.

[17] Ibid., 197.

[18] Ibid., 149-152.

between a: 1. Democratic polity with rights bearing citizens participating in governance; 2. A free economy (in which the state is not the chief economic actor, even as intervention is necessary for economic regulation); and 3. A vibrant public moral culture.[19]

Pope John Paul II would contribute, based on his deeply personalist philosophy, that persons were needed for both a democracy and a market to function in an ethical manner. Moral persons are required so that society functions well and flourishes according to these principles. Pope Benedict and Pope Francis would later build on this foundation and contribute in their own distinctive styles to these truths of the human person. In fact, Weigel, in his definitive biography of Pope Saint John Paul II, *Witness to Hope*, in describing the drafting of *Centesimus Annus,* speaks of economics from the perspective of personhood, from the philosophy of the person as a moral actor. Weigel continues by referring directly to the Encyclical by stating: "It would attempt a description of the 'economic person' as one dimension of the 'acting person,' the moral agent created with intelligence and free will, both of which have something to do with economic life."[20] Astoundingly, the human person may be regarded as economically distinctive in his or her particularity, as a moral protagonist uniquely defined by the entrepreneurship with regards to his or her contribution to the common good.

---

[19] Ibid., 209.

[20] G. WEIGEL, *Witness To Hope: The Biography of Pope John Paul II*, Harper Collins, 1999, 613. Cf. JOHN PAUL II, *Centessimus annus*, Encyclical, 1991, #13.

## 9.5 THE UNIVERSAL DECLARATION ON HUMAN RIGHTS (1948)

A poignant apex in the realm of political communities relating to each other in communion came in the Twentieth Century in the year 1948, when on December 10 in Paris, France the United Nations drafted the milestone document the *Universal Declaration on Human Rights*. For the first time in a universal document created by diverse nations, creeds, and ethnicities, the world was able to come together and agree philosophically upon the dignity and rights due to every created human person. The universal document exemplifies a profound and illuminative convergence of the best of modern philosophical accomplishments, post-ideology in the language of rights. Similarly, Professor David Walsh's illumination of the person as "before being" reflects the sacred and transcendent value of every human person, and the rights that they must be accorded due to this dignity."[21] Without rights there would be tyranny in the political community, and one could also add tyranny in the Church. All of the modern Popes since Leo XIII have subsequently appropriated the language of rights, which manifests both the interpersonal communion within the Church and the relationship to secular authority and constitutional governments.

The French Revolution certainly saw the abominable murders of religious persons and priests, as the Church was brought to her knees; nevertheless, from the ashes of these unspeakable crimes

---

[21] D. WALSH, *Politics of the Person as the Politics of Being*, 2016, 187-205.

against Catholic persons, the human person does emerge out of the ashes. Yes, Napoleon rose as a Dictator in France, but so also the United States of America also rose from the same philosophical and political principles as the French Revolution.

German sociologist Hans Joas, in his *The Sacredness of the Human Person: A New Genealogy of Human Rights* (2013), analyzes the genesis and history of human rights beginning with the French Revolution, wherein he observes that the narrative of human rights as anti-religious is mythical, and he argues that the proponents of this view are likely "reactionary clerics, aristocrats, and allied intellectuals."[22] The fact that the ties were loosened and cut between the throne and the altar does did not in any manner lessen its religious intensity, as the French Revolutionaries sang the *Te Deum* and had objects blessed as often as possible.[23] Joas notes that scholars have become increasingly more skeptical about the Enlightenment's perceived constitutive a-religiosity or anti-religiosity,[24] as he argues that the French Revolution bears the seeds of reforming Catholicism and not abolishing it. Joas, a French sociologist, refers to the French *Declaration of the Rights of Man and of the Citizen* (1789) which, is the product of the earliest phase of the Revolution and refers to human rights as "sacred."[25] Walsh makes a similar point on rights when he states that the concept for Hobbes and Locke was not subjective, but

[22] H. JOAS, *The Sacredness of the Human Person*, Georgetown University Press, 2013, 11.

[23] Ibid., 12.

[24] Ibid., 15.

[25] Ibid., 16.

rather rooted in the transcendent.[26] It is known that the Americans in Paris, particularly Thomas Jefferson and Benjamin Franklin, played a massive role in the production of this French Declaration.[27] Upon this foundation, and together with religion, Joas argues for the support of the sacredness and inviolable dignity of every human person against the depersonalizing forces of modernity.[28] Joas then makes the illumined proposal for the "sacralization of the person" so as to protect and enshrine this reality in modern constitutional society.[29]

The principle reason for this project, which is in the full acceptance of the premise that ethics must precede ontology, lies in the truth that the dialogical principle is essential to the relational structure upon which the human person is created, and that this is not only a truth of philosophy, but a truth for the ecclesial person as well. The first obligation of the human person, in the order of philosophy, is to responsibly accept that their being is constituted by the other and that they are obliged to enter into the horizon of responsibility and thus become a contributing part of the political community. Every person is an "I" and every other person, regardless of race, ethnicity or creed, particularly within the political community is a "thou." The collective political community, according to Walsh, is a transcendent force and always outlives the particular person. Every person becomes a sacramental presence to the other within the

---

[26] D. WALSH, *The Priority of the Person: Political, Philosophical and Historical Discoveries*, University of Notre Dame, 2020, 46-51.

[27] H. JOAS, *The Sacredness of the Human Person*, 19.

[28] Ibid., 31-32.

[29] Ibid., 37.

context of community. The French throne did not enable the human person to be fully developed within the *polis*. The sacredness of the political community is not simply rooted in the nation defined in itself apart from the persons that comprise it; rather, it's sacredness is realized only in the capacity of the authority to reverence and actualize the freedom that is the person's right as a moral agent.

## 9.6 Faith through the Sacramentality of Personhood

Relationality is the highest *preambula fidei* (natural preamble to the act of faith). Relationality serves as the highest natural proof that a Trinitarian God is reasonable. When human persons are together, they establish laws amongst themselves that they all agree upon so that they may all operate within the zone of responsibility and remain ethical in their relationships with each other. When one person freely decides to separate themselves from this zone of responsibility, and step outside of the law, prison is the dire consequence, and freedom is lost. Similarly, on the supernatural level, if the *biological hypostasis* chooses to not become an *ecclesial hypostasis*, and thus receive an enduring ontology into eternity, heaven is lost, and no ontology is given that endures. The political community is called to become a family and thus mirrors the Trinitarian family of God. Persons come to higher and transcendental beliefs by establishing themselves in trustful communion with other persons. The Church is thus capable of illumining the *polis*.

## 9.7 PASTORAL ILLUSTRATION – SACRAMENTAL PRESENCE OF THE OTHER

We recall a beautiful story about how a believer in God came to help a non-believer in God arrive at the beginning of faith in God. The non-believing person told the believing person over dinner that he needed something tangible so that he may believe. The believer then asked the non-believer the question: Do you believe that I believe in God? The non-believer answered *yes*. The believing man then told the non-believing man that this is where faith starts, in seeing faith in another person. The believing man then walked with the non-believing man outside into the night sky and the former asked the latter to look up at the stars. God separated those stars the believer said. The believer then explained a bit more to the non-believer about the Father's creation, and how those stars have led him to the presence of the divine in his spiritual life. The believer in this story was a sacramental presence to the non-believer through his personhood. Without seeing the faith of the believer, the person, the non-believer would not have been able to look up at the stars and possibly think of God. The non-believer needed the sacramental presence of a person to provide him with the tangibility he desired, the stars were too far away, not personal enough, too distant. This is how the other is often brought to belief and religion in a liberal culture, through the presence of the other, through the presence of the person who is living the belief and passing it to the other in some manner. Nothing is forced, every person has a choice, and the choice is free, to step into belief and religion, or to live outside of it. The believer received a letter years latter from the non-believer, who was now a believer. The newly converted believer stated in the letter of gratitude that the encounter over dinner had led him to belief in God.

## 9.8 Conclusion

Ethics indeed precedes ontology, but at the same time ethics must follow ontology. The ethics that follows ontology becomes an ethics that is rooted in religion, in particular the Holy Eucharist, the place where ontology is granted. In the Holy Eucharist, where the believer is first ordered toward the vertical worship of God, the horizontal relationships of the "I" and the "Thou" in the context of the Eucharist only grow deeper. The believer becomes immersed ever more deeply simultaneously in both self-awareness, and service, as bonds of trust grow when believers share faith with each other through personal vulnerability and dialogical communion. The Holy Eucharist, enriched by the offerings of philosophy and science that are continually brought there, and illumined by the supernatural virtue of faith, in this real life place of practical knowledge, leading deeper and deeper into the inexorable mystery of the person among persons in God, enlivened by the symbiotic complementarity of reason and faith.

# Chapter Ten

# Pope Benedict XVI and Pope Francis: Metaphysic of Love and the Human Response to Divine Revelation

"You shall love the Lord, your God, with all your heart, with all your soul and with all your mind, this is the greatest and the first commandment. The second is like it, you shall love your neighbor as yourself."

(Matthew 22:37-39)

As mentioned in Part One Chapter Two, both Pope Benedict and Pope Francis; this is seen in their respective Encyclicals *Deus Caritas Est* (2006), *Spe Salvi* (2007), *Caritas in Veritate* (2009) and *Lumen Fidei* (2013), along with the Apostolic Exhortations *Evangelii Gaudium* (2013), *Gaudete et Exsultate* (2018), along with the Encyclicals *Fratelli Tutti* (2020) and *Dilexit Nos* (2024), which have contributed to the emergence of a theological methodology. In this Chapter we will trace these pontificates along the lines of a turn to the person with Pope Benedict's *Caritas in Veritate* (2009), and Pope Francis's *Lumen Fidei* (2013), which connected the beginning of the Pontificate of Francis with the foundation that Pope Benedict had established, providing the theological foundation for Pope Francis's Magisterial contribution.

## 10.1 Spe Salvi (2007)

Pope Benedict, in this Encyclical, speaks of the inner disclosure of meaning occurring in the life of the human person.[1] He emphasizes that there is no actual relationship with God but the one that is accessed by the interiority of the human person.[2] The Pope states: "To be a person is to love, for we are scarcely persons to the extent that we love."[3] Benedict states that love captures us and seizes us because we know that it is transcendent to our person. Because we are captured by love we then love the other person in a manner that the other affectively experiences our love as if it were particularly destined solely and uniquely for him or her.[4] Echoing David Walsh, Pope Benedict states that "each one must be for us the whole world."[5] We see this contribution in *Spe Salvi*, where we see the account of hope illustrated, and are reminded that to be a person is to "live within the eschatological tension of the already and the not yet."[6] As eschatology had been a long-standing occupation of Ratzinger the theologian, as Pope he discovers the language that we do not hope for the eschaton, but actually live within its assurance.[7] The Pope's exegesis of Hebrews 11:1, "faith is the substance (*hypostasis*) of things hoped for; the proof of things not seen" provides us

---

[1] BENEDICT XVI, *Spe Salvi,* Encyclical, 2007, #11.

[2] Ibid.

[3] Ibid., #19.

[4] Ibid.

[5] Ibid., #27.

[6] Ibid., #9.

[7] Ibid. #12.

with a rich insight into this perennial philosophical thicket of *hypostasis* and substance. Within this Encyclical, Benedict reminds us that *hypostasis* may never be considered as a technical term, and that the inability to understand its existential importance has led us to the inability to access the interior life in any language other than subjectivity.[8] Benedict, in turn, understands the meaning of *hypostasis* from the Letter to the Hebrews to mean that the human person "already possesses" what he or she awaits.[9] *Ousia* (substance), the Pope states, on the other hand, cannot be the same as life itself, because it does not go beyond this life, it is not what sustains the life within which we live,[10] which vindicates the entirety of our project in this one declaration. Furthermore, the hope that eschatology brings, both within the Church and within society, protects the Social Doctrine of the Church from becoming ideological.[11]

## 10.2 CARITAS IN VERITATE (2009)

The lines of Catholic social thought in *Caritas in Veritate* richly illumine personhood. At the time of our second project in 2009, *Caritas in Veritate* was promulgated, and we overlooked it and dismissed it as not pertaining to ontology, relegating it only to the social teaching of the Church, and thus irrelevant to our project at that time, which pertained to the ontology of personhood and

[8] Ibid.

[9] Ibid.

[10] Ibid., #10.

[11] Ibid., #20.

communion. Seventeen years later, Professor Walsh has helped us bridge a gap and see a correspondence in an understanding of personhood that we would have never have been able to see from a purely ecclesiological perspective, as in hindsight we needed his contribution so to see the full splendor of the philosophical person in society held before us. Pope Benedict in this Encyclical reflects on the Social Doctrine of the Church from Leo XIII through Pope Saint John Paul II, speaking of an open system, with a "dynamic faithfulness to the light received", and then "illuminating with an unchanging light."[12] To the challenges of our time Pope Benedict recommends an integral "humanistic synthesis."[13]

Also important to our project is the Pope's insistence in *Caritas in Vertitate* on a metaphysical interpretation of the unity of human persons with relationality as the primary category.[14] Pope Benedict cites his predecessor Pope Saint John Paul II in his *Centessimus Annus* (1991), regarding an "important interdisciplinary dimension"[15] which allows faith, theology, metaphysics and science to come together in a collaborative way in the service of humanity.[16] In fact, Pope Benedict frequently references Pope Saint Paul VI, in his Encyclical Letter *Populorum Progressio* (1967), as he observes that Pope Paul VI saw, upon reflection, a lack of wisdom which led to the "underdevelopment" of the Social Doctrine of the Church, and that a

---

[12] BENEDICT XVI, *Caritas in Veritate*, Encyclical, 2009, #12.

[13] Ibid., #70.

[14] Ibid.,, #55.

[15] Ibid., #69. Cf. JOHN PAUL II, *Centessimus Annus*, Encyclical, #42.

[16] Ibid., #31.

"clear vision" a "guiding synthesis" was still needed.[17] It is at this point that Walsh's understanding of person enters, to deepen the Church's dialogical engagement with society by using the natural language of rights so as to invite it to the transcendence beyond nature and into the supernatural hope to which it is called. According to Walsh, in this Encyclical by Pope Benedict we see "the full development of the human person that is held before us" as Benedict states "that it is the truth filled love (*caritas in veritate*) from which authentic development proceeds."[18] Here we can see the ontology of love from which any understanding of the person must be rooted before we speak of the moral life of the person in society, illumined by the Social Doctrine of the Church. The full development of the human person, according to Pope Benedict, is the human person becoming a partaker in the divine life, which in turn will illumine all of the structures of modern civilization.[19]

In Chapter Fourteen of David Walsh's *The Priority of the Person* (2020),[20] he both captures and reflects upon how both Pope Benedict and Pope Francis understood the great challenges that the secular world represents. The Church is trying to speak to a world that has not only lost its faith, but is no longer searching for it, as God is increasingly ignored, a lack of interest.[21] Walsh observes that Pope

---

[17] Ibid., 31. Cf. Pope Paul VI, *Populorum Progressio*, Encyclical, #40, #85.

[18] D. WALSH, *The Priority of the Person*, 279. Cf. BENEDICT XVI, *Caritas in Veritate,* # 79.

[19] Ibid., 280.

[20] D. WALSH, *The Priority of the Person*, 269.

[21] Ibid.

Benedict advanced theological personalism further than what he did prior in his history as a theologian. For example, for Benedict, Walsh observes that the Church will change the world neither by separating from it, nor from submitting to it, but only by "revealing the eschatological secret buried within it."[22] Even in an agnostic world, there is a fundamental agreement that human rights need to be protected with dignity and respect. People agree that tolerance may be undermined if it is extended to the intolerant.[23] In any situation of intolerance, human rights cry out for a transcendent basis. The question must be asked: From where does a human person receive their infinite worth? Pope Benedict, according to Walsh, had been engaged for decades in searching to make theological and philosophical language more transparent, and indirectly working from the notion that the language of substance was defective in its ability to address this transparency through language.[24] Pope Benedict, building on his predecessors, took the project toward personhood one step further by "thinking within the language of relation."[25] As the Church's social teaching has developed, Walsh has discovered in Pope Benedict a manner of speaking to the world in a social language, but at the same time "looking toward the movement beyond it."[26] Walsh, a political philosopher immersed in the reality of the world with every breath of his thought, discovered the depth of brilliance in the

---

[22] Ibid., 270.
[23] Ibid., 271-272.
[24] Ibid., 273.
[25] Ibid.
[26] Ibid., 274.

practical relevance of the papal teaching of Pope Benedict, and in him found a convergence with his own philosophical thought.

According to Walsh, the truth that Pope Benedict conveyed in this his last Encyclical was that "self-transcendence is the authentic meaning of social progress." A Civilization of Love is fulfilled when it is understood as the only appropriate way of addressing persons, who are always more than what they have said or done.[27] Walsh observes: "Persons, as the only genuine ends-in-themselves, are, thus, the only adequate end of civilization itself.[28]" This language from the Church that is accessible to the contemporary world marks a significant achievement according to Walsh.[29] For example, the human person is a steward of the earth's resources and is called to foster a "human ecology" that will lead to an "environmental ecology."[30] The call to be stewards of creation is therefore here understood through the lens of personhood. The reality that we are all one human family is located within the category of relation.[31]

Walsh captures the metaphysical import of Benedict's contribution in this Encyclical wherein Pope Benedict states:

> Inclusion-in-relation of all individuals and peoples within the one community of the human family, built in solidarity on the fundamental values of justice and peace, is a perspective illumined in a striking way by the relationship between

[27] Ibid.

[28] Ibid.

[29] Ibid.

[30] Ibid., 281. citing BENEDICT XVI, *Caritas in Veritate*, #51.

[31] Ibid.

> the Persons of the Trinity within the one divine Substance. The Trinity is absolute unity insofar as the three divine Persons are pure relationality. The reciprocal transparency among the divine Persons is total and the bond between each of them complete, since they constitute a unique and absolute unity.[32]

Pope Benedict continues by stating that God desires to incorporate us into the reality of this communion. "Relationships between human beings throughout history cannot but be enriched by reference to the divine model."[33] Furthermore, Benedict continues, "In the light of the revealed mystery of the Trinity, we understand that true openness does not mean the loss of individual identity but profound interpretation. This also emerges from the common human experiences of love and truth."[34] Walsh astutely observes that the "analogue" for persons in communion relating to each other is the relationship between the Persons of the Trinity with the one divine Substance.[35] "A community of persons is one in which each, far from losing his or her identity, finds it enhanced immeasurably."[36] Benedict continues:

---

[32] BENEDICT XVI, *Caritas in Veritate*, #54. Cf. D. WALSH, *Priority of the Person*, 281.

[33] Ibid., #58.

[34] Ibid.

[35] D. WALSH, *Priority of the Person*, 281.

[36] Ibid.

> The Christian revelation of the unity of the human race presupposes a *metaphysical interpretation of the "humanum" in which relationality is an essential element.* Other cultures and religions teach brotherhood and peace and are therefore of enormous importance to integral human development. Some religious and cultural attitudes, however, do not fully embrace the principle of love and truth and therefore end up retarding or even obstructing authentic human development. There are certain religious cultures in the world today that do not oblige men and women to live in communion but rather cut them off from one another in a search for individual well-being.[37]

Walsh understands that Pope Benedict does not have a fully developed political theory, but clearly assists in defending the person from the "devaluation that technological mastery poses."[38] Pope Benedict continues, "the development of peoples is intimately linked to the development of individuals."[39] The Pope continues by stating that "we all build our own 'I' on the basis of a 'self' which is given to us. Not only are other persons outside of our control, but each one of us is outside of his or her control."[40] Walsh observes that the problem Pope Benedict confronts is the problem of the "reign of technology"[41] over the human person, and Walsh reminds us, rooted in this

---

[37] BENEDICT XVI, *Caritas in Veritate*, #55.

[38] D. WALSH, *Priority of the Person*, 282.

[39] POPE BENEDICT XVI, *Caritas in Veritate*, #68.

[40] Ibid., Cf. Walsh, *Priority of the Person*, 282.

[41] BENEDICT XVI, *Caritas in Veritate*, #32.

developed thinking of Benedict, that an "absolute limit to this control must be the interiority of the person in him-or herself."[42] "In the end is the mystery of the person that encompasses the mystery of knowledge and of love. There is no higher reality than the person for there is nothing higher than God."[43] Walsh continues in his observation of Pope Benedict's contribution to advancing personhood by stating: "The only difficulty is that we still talk about persons as if they are part of the order of things. In Benedict's perceptive formulation we use the language of substance to identify persons who have already sacrificed their substance. Knowledge and love are movements of pure relation where the person has forgotten him -or herself. It is thus difficult to say what the person is who has always disappeared in what each has said or done."[44] Walsh concludes:

> Benedict's instincts have led him to pay attention to the great modern thinkers, but he has usually ended by accepting conventional characterizations of them as falling short of the Christian horizon. As a consequence, neither he nor his predecessor has been able to exploit the full potential of the modern philosophical revolution. Tantalizing suggestions as to what might be possible, however, do become visible. It is remarkable, for example, how frequently Benedict returned to Kant to probe the Christian core of the "rational" faith the latter puts in place of "ecclesiastical faith." Yet Benedict does

[42] D. WALSH, *Priority of the Person*, 282.
[43] Ibid.
[44] Ibid., 282-283.

not quite see that this implies, whatever Kant's mischaracterization of historical Christianity, that Kant nevertheless sought its purer, more interior, affirmation.[45]

## 10.3 Lumen Fidei (2013)

In this, the first Encyclical of Pope Francis, Walsh argues that the Pope discovered that "longing for an unattainable God" is in itself a "mode of attainment."[46] "The loss of God may be stated, but it can only be stated because God has not been lost." This Walsh argues is the greatest response to the drama of atheism, that "the God who is perceived as absent is the one who is help with the deepest inwardness." "My God, My God, why have you forsaken me?"[47] "Can transcendence be held in any other way than through transcendence?"[48] Walsh observes, "The circuit that had begun with the opening of the reflection in *Deus Caritas Est* (2005) and then taught us that we are saved by hope, *Spe Salvi* (2007), seemingly reaching what seemed a conclusion in locating charity within the truth, *Caritas in Veritate* (2009), now becomes a reality in *Lumen Fidei* ( 2013), which Walsh accurately describes as a bridge Encyclical between Pope Benedict and Pope Francis. Walsh characterizes this work as a "breakthrough" wherein we no longer speak *about* "the person and the imperative of conceiving human life within the category of relation"

[45] Ibid., 283.

[46] Ibid., 284.

[47] Ibid.

[48] Ibid.

but on the *actual implementation* of the reality of this theory "as a meditation on the light of faith that makes all faith possible."[49] "Faith, because it emerges as a truth claim, already strains against the presumption that there is no truth."[50] Walsh continues: in his reflection on *Lumen fidei*:

> The great breakthrough is that where previously Ratzinger-Benedict had felt compelled to defend truth, even faith in truth, now he could unfold truth as its own movement of faith. The shift to the relational perspective of the person has been completed. And that meant that faith could be contemplated entirely from within the movement by which it is constituted, without the slightest concession to the subjective character of its conviction. Interiority had been banished when the transition has been made to the reality within which it is located. We do not keep faith, for faith is what keeps us.[51]

With *Lumen Fidei*, Pope Benedict and Pope Francis together usher us in to speak of faith as opening up a "vast horizon" given by the "great joy of believing."[52] It becomes apparent that trust is most appropriately placed "in a person who is trustworthy, who is

[49] D. WALSH, *The Priority of the Person*, 284.

[50] Ibid.

[51] Ibid.

[52] FRANCIS, *Lumen Fidei*, Encyclical, 2013, #5. Cf. D. Walsh, *The Priority of the Person*, 285.

trustworthiness as such."[53] We come to find in this Encyclical that "meaning points comprehensively toward the person who comprehensively reveals it," as Walsh observes in the call of Abraham described in the First Chapter of the Encyclical, as the example of the call not being a general possibility, but the possibility of the call for a "specific individual."[54] In fact this First Chapter of *Lumen Fidei* begins with the "Thou" who "calls us by name."[55] In our opinion, with an implicit nod to Zizioulas, faith is described as a "remembrance of the future (*memoria futuri*)," thus capturing a proper eschatology, and the understanding of how it is bound with hope.[56] With a reference to Martin Buber, the Encyclical states that "Faith by its very nature demands renouncing the immediate possession which sight would appear to offer; it is an invitation to turn to the source of the light, while respecting the mystery of a countenance which will unveil itself personally in its own time."[57]

The "We" of the community, Walsh states, is "constituted for the journey of faith in time."[58] The Encyclical states, "The individual's act of faith finds its place within the community, with the common 'we' of the people, who in faith are like a single person."[59] "The self-awareness of the believer now expands because of the presence of another; it now lives in the other and thus, in love, life takes on a

---

[53] D. WALSH, *The Priority of the Person*, 285.

[54] Ibid. Cf. FRANCIS, *Lumen Fidei*, #8-#22.

[55] Ibid., #8.

[56] Ibid., #9.

[57] Ibid., #13.

[58] D. WALSH, *The Priority of the Person*, 286.

[59] FRANCIS, *Lumen Fidei*, #14.

whole new breadth."[60] Walsh observes that the superiority of faith lies not in its "subjective conviction" but in the connection with truth that is built into it."[61] Drawing on the modern Austro-British philosopher Ludwig Wittgenstein (1889-1951) the Encyclical states: "One who loves realizes that love is an experience of truth, that it opens our eyes to see reality in a new way, in union with the beloved."[62] "The search that each must personally undertake now reaches its goal in the disclosure of God as a person who has all along been present in the call."[63] Walsh continues:

> The personal encounter with the Other opens to all others who are loved in the same way, without limit or condition, and thereby move definitively away from anything merely singular or private. The truth of love and the love of truth underpin the common good. It unites all who are seeking, whether in science or in other religions or in theology itself, for it is a subordination to the call of truth that each has heard in his or her own uniquely personal way.[64]

---

[60] Ibid., #21. Cf. D. WALSH, *The Priority of the Person*, 286.

[61] D. WALSH, *The Priority of the Person*, 286.

[62] FRANCIS, *Lumen Fidei*, #27. "The explanation of the connection between faith and certainty put forward by the philosopher Ludwig Wittgenstein is well known. For Wittgenstein, believing can be compared to the experience of falling in love: it is something subjective which cannot be proposed as a truth valid for everyone." Cf. D. WALSH, *The Priority of the Person*, 287.

[63] D. WALSH, *The Priority of the Person*, 287.

[64] Ibid.

How helpful it will be to a seminarian in the Discipleship Stage of Priestly Formation, or for a Catholic undergraduate, to apply theology to the growth of his or her philosophical knowledge by using this Encyclical as a source for learning the relationship shared between the two disciplines of philosophy and theology as we propose that *Lumen Fidei* be used as an actual philosophical text in the classroom. As the emerging disciple reads that "Joined to hearing, seeing then becomes a form of following Christ, and faith appears as a process of gazing, in which our eyes grow accustomed to peering into the depths."[65] All God's "light" is concentrated in Jesus who is described here as "luminous life." "There is no human experience, no journey of man to God, which cannot be taken up, illumined and purified by this light."[66] Pope Francis finally describes "Interpersonal knowledge as the culmination of faith affirms the validity of knowledge."[67] God can no longer be "reduced to an object,"[68] but rather "He is a subject who makes himself known and perceived in an interpersonal relationship. Right faith orients reason to open itself to the light that comes from God, so that reason, guided by the love of the truth, can come to a deeper knowledge of God."[69]

---

[65] FRANCIS, *Lumen Fidei*, #30.

[66] Ibid., #35.

[67] D. WALSH, *The Priority of the Person*, 287.

[68] POPE FRANCIS, *Lumen Fidei*, #36.

[69] Ibid.

## 10.4 Evangelii Gaudium (2013)

Pope Francis, in his Apostolic Exhortation *Evangelii Gaudium* (2013), invites each individual Christian in every place, at this very moment to either a "renewed personal encounter with Jesus Christ," or at least an openness to letting him encounter them."[70] He invites all of the faithful into an "encounter, or a renewed encounter with God's love, which blossoms into an enriching friendship, liberated from our narrowness and self-absorption."[71] Pope Francis refers back to Pope Benedict in his Encyclical Letter *Deus Caritas Est* wherein Benedict stated, "Being a Christian is not the result of an ethical choice or a lofty idea, but the encounter with an event, a person, which gives life a new horizon and a decisive direction."[72] Pope Francis then develops in this Exhortation, which develops the theological vision of his Pontificate, in the context of the social demands of the Gospel.[73] In the Fourth Chapter of this Exhortation, Pope Francis calls the Church to the communal awareness of the special concern for the poor;[74] the evaluation of structures of economic policies with regard to how they are called to contribute to the common good;[75] concern for the vulnerable;[76] and for peace within society.[77]

---

[70] FRANCIS, *Evangelii Gaudium*, Apostolic Exhortation 2013, #3.

[71] Ibid., #8.

[72] Ibid., #7.

[73] Ibid., #176-237.

[74] Ibid., #197-201.

[75] Ibid., #202-208.

[76] Ibid., #209-216.

[77] Ibid., #217-221.

With an astute use of philosophy, Pope Francis uses the concept that "time is greater than space" seeing that "time has to do with fullness, as an expression of the horizon which constantly opens before us." As people live within time, they live within "the greater brighter horizon of the utopian future as the final cause which draws us to itself. Here we see a first principle for progress in building a people: time is greater than space."[78] Pope Francis, in his search for unity among people and societies again philosophically observes that "unity prevails over conflict." The Pope states that: "Conflict cannot be ignored or concealed, it has to be faced." At the same time, when we become "trapped in conflict, we lose our perspective, our horizons shrink and reality itself begins to fall apart."[79]

Finally, and also closely related to this project, insofar as it bears Kantian likeness, is his philosophical assertion that "realties are more important than ideas."[80] Pope Francis states that ideas must not become detached from realities. He calls us to reject "the various means of masking reality: angelic forms of purity, dictatorships of relativism, empty rhetoric, objectives more ideal than real, brands of ahistorical fundamentalism, ethical systems bereft of kindness, and intellectual discourse bereft of wisdom."[81] The principle of the Incarnation of the Word demands, according to Pope Francis, that "realities are greater than ideas,"[82] and we gently wonder here if Immanuel Kant did not maintain the same.

---

[78] Ibid., #222.

[79] Ibid., #226-230.

[80] Ibid., #231.

[81] Ibid, #231.

[82] Ibid., #233.

As we have made our claim that truth is discovered primarily in the Holy Eucharist, and that participation there is the epistemic source for our knowledge, as noted with the contribution of Metropolitan Zizioulas, Pope Francis affirms this approach to epistemology by stating, "There is no need then, to be overly obsessed with limited and particular questions. We constantly have to broaden our horizons and see the greater good which will benefit us all."[83] From the context of Ecclesiology, this principle should be sure to prove helpful in future endeavors towards Christian Unity.

## 10.5 Gaudete et Exultate (2018)

With Francis's Apostolic Exhortation *Gaudete et Exsultate* (2018), the Pope calls us to holiness in today's world, by way of addressing two subtle enemies of holiness, Gnosticism and Pelagianism. He describes Gnosticism as a "set of ideas and bits of information which are meant to console and enlighten, but which ultimately keep one imprisoned in his or her own thoughts and feelings."[84] Continuing by describing this contemporary heresy as "an intellect without God and without flesh," he states: "Thanks be to God, throughout the history of the Church, it has always been clear that a person's perfection is measured not by the information or knowledge they possess, but by the depth of their charity."[85] Pope

[83] Ibid., #235.

[84] POPE FRANCIS, *Gaudete et exultate*, Apostolic Exhortation, 2018, #36.

[85] Ibid., #37.

Francis, while solidifying our argument that knowledge should always be centered in the Eucharistic community, becomes even stronger on this point by stating that "Gnosticism is one of the most sinister ideologies because, while unduly exalting knowledge or specific experience, it considers its own vision of reality to be perfect."[86] For Francis this is an approach to doctrine devoid of mystery.[87]

Continuing in the same Exhortation, the Pope speaks of the contemporary heresy of Pelagianism. Francis teaches that the same power the Gnostics attribute to the human intellect, the Pelagians attribute to the human will, that is to personal effort.[88] Even though Pelagians speak of God's grace, they "ultimately trust only in their own powers and feel superior to others because they observe certain rules or remain intransigently faithful to a particular Catholic style."[89] For the contemporary Pelagian, "ultimately the lack of a heartfelt and prayerful acknowledgement of our limitations prevents grace from working more effectively within us, for no room is left for bringing about the potential good that is part of a sincere and genuine journey of growth."[90] The Pelagian, or Semi-Pelagian, in contemporary form, gives the idea that all things are possible by the human will, and they therefore lack humility.[91] Both of these heresies become beacons of warning and assist in guiding us toward a faithful epistemology discovered within the context of communion.

---

[86] Ibid., #40.

[87] Ibid.

[88] Ibid., #47-48.

[89] Ibid., #49.

[90] Ibid., #50.

[91] Ibid., #49.

## 10.6 Fratelli Tutti (2020)

Pope Francis converges with Professor Walsh in his understanding of the predominance of human rights within a society, when reflecting on the Parable of the Good Samaritan he states:

> The Parable does not indulge in abstract morality, nor is it a message merely social and ethical. It speaks to us of an essential and forgotten aspect of our common humanity: we were created for fulfillment that can only be found in love. We cannot be indifferent to suffering; we cannot allow anyone to go through life as an outcast. Instead, we should feel indignant, challenged to emerge from our comfortable isolation and to be challenged by our contact with human suffering. This is the meaning of dignity.[92]

Francis continues in the same Encyclical by observing:

> It frequently becomes clear that in practice human rights are not equal for all. Respect for those rights is a preliminary condition for a country's social and economic development. When the dignity of the human person is respected, and his or her rights recognized or guaranteed, creativity and independence thrive and the creativity of the human personality is released through actions that further the Common Good.[93]

---

[92] FRANCIS, *Fratelli Tutti*, Encyclical, 2020, #68.

[93] Ibid., #22.

## 10.7 Dilexit Nos (2024)

To conclude his Pontificate, Pope Francis provided us with the Encyclical *Dilexit Nos*, which is a journey into the human and divine heart of Christ. In this final Encyclical before his death, Pope Francis plunges deeper into the mystery of love in the heart of the human person than we have seen in any previous Magisterial document. Here the Pope describes the heart as the "locus of sincerity, where deceit and disguise have no place."[94] The heart is the part of us that "indicates our true intentions, what we really think, believe, and desire, the secrets that we tell no one: in a word the naked truth about ourselves. It is the part of us that is neither appearance or illusion, but is instead authentic, real, entirely who we are."[95] "Despite our every attempt to appear as something we are not, our heart is the ultimate judge, not of what we show or hide from others, but of who we truly are."[96] The Pope reflects on how the contemporary person, "bombarded by technology" "risks losing their center, the center of their very selves."[97] It is love alone that leads us to a deeper self-awareness as we are immersed in God, and so the journey into God, into the other, and deeper into ourselves become simultaneous as, "the failure to make room for the heart, as distinct from our own human powers and passions viewed in isolation from one another, has resulted in the stunting of the idea of a personal center, in which

---

[94] POPE FRANCIS, *Dilexit Nos*, 2024, #5.

[95] Ibid.

[96] Ibid.

[97] Ibid., #9.

love, in the end, is the one reality that can unify all of the others."[98] Pope Francis states:

> In the heart of each person there is a mysterious connection between self-knowledge and openness to others, between the encounter with one's personal uniqueness and the willingness to give oneself to others. We become ourselves only to the extent that we acquire the ability to acknowledge others, while only those who can acknowledge and accept themselves are then able to encounter others.[99]

## 10.8 Pope Leo XIV (2025)

On May 8, 2025, Pope Leo XIV emerged on the *loggia* of the Basilica of Saint Peter in Rome as the first Pope in the history of Roman Catholic Church to be born in the United States of America. It was this election, and the choice of the name which inspired our writing of this text so as to assist our new Pope in building on the foundation and Magisterium that emerged in the Pontificate of Pope Leo XIII, the first modern Pope, and will continue through this emerging Pontificate. What the Church is sure to find, is that the *sacramentality of personhood* will be even further illumined and developed. This Pontiff, born in the land where freedom, justice and equality were first historically realized, in the birth of a new democratic and modern nation, the

[98] Ibid., #10.
[99] Ibid., #18.

United States of America, now leads the world in his person into a deeper discovery of these same truths. Furthermore, our new Pope is a Shepherd with a missionary heart with an experience forged by the encounter with the other, especially God's holy poor, which were fundamental in the formation of his priestly and episcopal journey.

www.ingramcontent.com/pod-product-compliance
Lightning Source LLC
LaVergne TN
LVHW040217110826
845146LV00005B/1317